APPLE
Cookbook

Olwen Woodier

Storey Publishing

The mission of Storey Publishing is to serve our customers by publishing practical information that encourages personal independence in harmony with the environment.

COVER DESIGN AND ILLUSTRATION BY Rob Johnson
COVER PHOTOS BY Giles Prett and Richard Busch
TEXT DESIGN BY Erin Lincourt
BOOK PRODUCTION BY Erin Lincourt and Jennifer Jepson Smith
ILLUSTRATIONS BY Elayne Sears
EDITED BY Sally Patterson and Dianne M. Cutillo
INDEXED BY Nan Badgett/word·a·bil·i·ty

The information in this book is true and complete to the best of our knowledge. All recommendations are made without guarantee on the part of the author or Storey Publishing. The author and publisher disclaim any liability in connection with the use of this information. For additional information, please contact Storey Publishing, 210 MASS MoCA Way, North Adams, MA 01247.

Note: Many of the food preservation procedures described in this book are subject to U.S. Department of Agriculture guidelines. Storey updates information upon publication of each edition and encourages readers to check for the most current standards by writing to Cooperative State Research, Education, and Extension Service, U.S. Department of Agriculture, Washington, D.C. 20250-0900; calling 202-720-7441; or by visiting the agency's Web site at www.csrees.usda.gov. You may also contact the Extension Service in your county. In Canada, contact Public Information Request Service, Agriculture and Agri-Food Canada, Sir John Carling Building, 930 Carling Avenue, Ottawa, Ontario K1A 0C5; 613-759-1000; or visit the agency's Web site at www.agr.gc.ca.

Storey books are available for special premium and promotional uses and for customized editions. For further information, please call 1-800-793-9396.

Apple Cookbook was first published as *The Apple Cookbook* in 1984. All of the information in the previous edition was reviewed and updated, and new recipes and information were added.

Printed in the United States by Versa Press
20 19 18 17 16 15 14

Library of Congress Cataloging-in-Publication Data

Woodier, Olwen, date.
  Apple cookbook / by Olwen Woodier.
      p.   cm.
  Originally published: Pownal, Vt.: Garden Way Pub., c1984.
  Includes index.
  ISBN 978-1-58017-389-6 (alk.paper)
  1. Cookery (Apples) I. Title.
TX813.A6 W657 2001
641.6'411-dc21   2001020211

CONTENTS

Acknowledgments

Apple Cookbook is dedicated to the women who know that cooking for friends and family is not about following recipes but adding an extra pinch of love to nurture soul as well as body: Joyse Woodier, my mother (who, at 92, still bakes almost daily and puts up jams); my daughter, Wendy Busch, and my longtime best friend Ann Kojis Ziff.

There are so many people who made this book possible that I cannot mention all of them, but special thanks go to:

My dear friends, family, colleagues, and orchardists for sharing your recipes and knowledge of apples.

Julia Stewart Daly, Public Relations Director of the U.S. Apple Association in McClean, Virginia, who introduced me to many people in the apple industry and verified apple facts.

Dr. Susan Brown, head pomologist at Cornell University's Department of Horticultural Sciences at the New York State Agricultural Experiment Station in Geneva, New York, who steered me through the complicated issue of germ plasm and the process of breeding hybrid apples.

Jim Law of Linden Vineyards in Linden, Virginia, for his expert review of sections of the manuscript regarding aspects of growing dwarf varieties and employing Integrated Pesticide Methods.

John and Martha Storey for their faith in revising *The Apple Cookbook* which, when first published in 1984, won a Tastemaker Award, now known as the James Beard Foundation KitchenAid Book Award.

Sally Patterson, my editor at Storey, who guided me through the revision manuscript, and editor Dianne M. Cutillo for her indefatigable spirit in shepherding the book through its final editing.

Designers Erin Lincourt and Jennifer Jepson Smith, copyeditor Arlene Bouras, and others at Storey Publishing who have been instrumental in this new edition.

APPLE
History

MAN HAS BEEN MUNCHING on apples for about 750,000 years, ever since the food gatherers of early Paleolithic times discovered sour, wild crab apples growing in the forests in Kazakhstan, Central Asia. Botanists now believe that this region holds the key to the genetic origins of the wild apples that are the ancestors of the apples we enjoy today.

When U.S. botanists visited Kazakhstan in 1989, they found large stands of ancient apple trees — trees that were 300 years old, 50 feet tall, and bearing large red apples. These trees of *Malus sieversii*, the wild species now believed to be the parent of all domesticated apples, were discovered in 1929 by Russian botanist Nikolai I. Vavilov.

Unfortunately, Vavilov's work in genetics led to his imprisonment during the Stalin era. He died in prison in 1943. His wonderful discovery was finally announced to the rest of the world by a former student and coworker of Vavilov's who, at the age of 80, felt the need to pass along the knowledge before it was too late to save the forests of ancient apple trees.

THE ORIGIN OF THE APPLE

On discovering the ancient wild apple groves in Central Asia, Nikolai Vavilov rejoiced:

"All around the city one could see a vast expanse of wild apples covering the foothills. One could see with his own eyes that this beautiful site was the origin of the cultivated apple."

Apples on the Move

The carbonized remains of apples unearthed in Asia Minor indicate that Neolithic farmers were cultivating wild apples around 8,000 years ago. Later, apples were carried as transportable food by migrating cultures. It is speculated that somewhere along the way *M. sieversii* hybridized with *M. orientalis* and *M. sylvestris*, two wild species producing small and very sour green apples.

There is recorded evidence from 1300 B.C. of apple orchards being planted by the Egyptians along the Nile Delta. The Greeks learned grafting techniques around 800 B.C., and by 200 B.C. the Romans were planting apple orchards in Britain.

Apples Settle in America

Colonists arriving in America found only four varieties of wild crab apples. However, the French, Dutch, German, and English all brought seeds from their homelands, and it wasn't long before apple trees were growing outside their rustic dwellings. The English colonists were the first to bring apple tree scions (shoots) to North America.

The first American orchard was planted in Boston in 1625 by William Blaxton, an English preacher. A few years later, orchards were established in the same area by John Winthrop and John Endicott, governors of the Bay Colony settlement.

In 1647, Peter Stuyvesant, governor of New Amsterdam (now New York), planted the first Dutch apple trees on his farm, The Bouwerie. The first commercial orchard was planted in Flushing, New York, in 1730.

Thousands of varieties of apple trees evolved during the 18th and 19th centuries when colonial farmers decided to plant apple seeds instead of acquiring young tree scions arriving from England and Europe. As the colonists moved from the Atlantic coast westward, they planted apple seeds along the way.

Favorably influenced by moderately cool winters, the colonists' apple crops flourished in the northern regions. Apples, just like autumn leaves, need the perfect marriage of temperatures — warm, sunny days and cool nights that occur in October — to show off their best qualities.

America's Number-One Fruit

Cultivated throughout the United States, apples are grown for commercial production in 36 states. The main apple-growing regions are Washington, New York, Michigan, Pennsylvania, California, and Virginia. These six states produce most of the country's annual apple crop, which totaled 254,217 million bushels in 2000. About one-third of the annual U.S. apple crop is processed into juice and canned, frozen, and dehydrated products. The average American eats 48.41 pounds of apples a year.

It's not only their year-round availability that makes apples so desirable in the United States; there are a host of other reasons why they're America's number one fruit:

- They are delicious, versatile, and easily portable.
- They are nutritious, providing satisfying bulk and few calories. (See page 130 for information on nutritional values.)
- They are 85 to 95 percent water, so if you put one into your pocket or lunch box, you can quench your thirst whenever the need arises.
- Their acid content acts as a natural mouth freshener, which makes apples a perfect ending to a meal.
- They are believed to have many other healthful properties. (See page 183 for further information.)

Apple Allure

When Eve was tempted by the serpent in the Garden of Eden to eat "of the tree which is forbidden," she "saw that the tree was good for food, and that it was pleasant to the eyes, and a tree to be desired to make one wise." No doubt she was also quite taken by the shape, color, and smell of this "fruit of the gods."

Imagine yourself picking up an apple for the very first time. Turn it around in your hand. If it's one of the russet apples, it will feel rough and dry, not at all like a red-on-yellow Empire with its satiny smooth and tender skin. Hold it to your nose and breathe deeply. The smooth-skinned Empire will have a delicate smell that is well contained by its smooth and slightly oily skin. The rough skin of a ripe russet, on the other hand, will exude a tantalizing fragrance.

Most of the perfume cells are concentrated in the skin of an apple. As the apple ripens, the cells give off a stronger aroma. That is why applesauce is most flavorful when made from apples with the skin left on and the best cider is made from the aromatic, tough-skinned russets.

Rosy pink applesauce gets its color from the flesh, not from the skin — unless the skin has been puréed with the flesh to become an integral part of the sauce. The pigments trapped in the skin cells are not released during cooking, crushing, or pressing, because those color cells are impossible to break.

Apple trees not only have taken the fancy of gods and mortals, they attract more than 30 species of birds and a variety of four-legged animals. There are birds that love to nest in the spreading branches. Many birds and beasts feast on the buds, bark, and leaves. The ripe, fallen apples are favored by porcupines, skunks, fox, and deer. Opossums, raccoons, and bears all climb the limbs to get at apple-laden branches.

Popular Orchard Varieties

Although hundreds of varieties of apples are grown in the United States, only 20 or so best-sellers are cultivated in the major commercial orchards. Commercial apples are chosen not for their wonderful taste but for their bountiful harvest; their suitability to mass planting, shipping, and long storage; and their resistance to diseases.

Apples in Season

The orchards are invaded by armies of apple pickers as early as July, but it is not until the cooler temperatures of September have touched this "fruit of immortality," as it was once called, that an apple takes on those crisp and crunchy qualities so important to orchardists and apple lovers. It is in autumn that a bite into a fresh-picked apple becomes a memorable experience; the apple spurts juice that is honey sweet and yet also spicily tart, and the flesh is so fragrantly mellow.

After December, these fall beauties come to us from controlled storage — somewhere between 32 and 36°F. This controlled atmosphere helps to maintain the crisp qualities of the fall-harvested apples for several months. Today, shoppers find that a reasonable selection of apples is available after the last of the fresh harvest disappears into cold storage. From January through June, most of us can find such good keepers as Braeburn, Fuji, Gala, Golden Delicious, Granny Smith, Ida Red, McIntosh, Red Delicious, and Rome Beauty. In fact, Granny Smith, Golden Delicious, and Red Delicious are now available to us year round.

Detailed descriptions of apple varieties may be found in Meet the Apples: Apple Varieties, pages 168–180.

Apple Breeding

The decline in the selection of apple varieties can be traced to the end of the 19th century and the advent of commercial orchards. After World War II, the decline was hastened by the horticultural practice of mass-planting only a few reliable varieties that met certain requirements, such as the ability to produce heavy crops, resist diseases, endure long-distance transportation, and last in long-term cold storage. Smooth, evenly colored skin and pleasing shape also factored into the equation. Other varieties were chosen because they were the best candidates for large-scale production of juice, sauce, and pie filling. While these qualities tip the scales in favor of popularity with commercial growers, they narrow the choice of varieties available to consumers, especially those who shop primarily in supermarkets.

Fortunately, apple breeders are constantly developing new varieties that have great growing qualities and taste delicious. Breeders develop new varieties by hybridizing (crossbreeding) two proven varieties.

The Lure of the New Hybrids

During the past 10 to 15 years, North America has witnessed an influx of new varieties. Some, such as Fuji, Braeburn, Gala, and Pink Lady, started out as imports from Japan, Australia, and New Zealand. However, because they have many desirable qualities that appeal to both growers and consumers, they have been mass planted throughout the United States. Today, most of these newcomers have reached their growth potential in U.S. orchards and are just beginning to swing into full production.

While pomologists (apple breeders) are primarily concerned with developing hybrid varieties that are resistant to the major apple diseases (scab, fire blight, mildew, and cedar apple rust), quality attributes are also stressed.

A number of modern-day apple varieties are endowed with sweet-tart, juicy, crisp flesh. For example, Honeycrisp, a hybrid cross between Macoun and Honeygold developed at the University of Minnesota in 1960, has aromatic, honey sweet, crisp flesh that maintains its outstanding texture and flavor during long-term storage. Jonagold, a cross between Jonathan and Golden Delicious, is a high-ranking apple in U.S. apple taste tests. Another hybrid offspring of Golden Delicious (crossed with Lady Williams) was developed more recently in Australia. Going by the name of Pink Lady, it is a crunchy, all-purpose apple with a mouthwatering, sweet-tart flavor. It made its consumer debut in October 2000.

Liberty, another hybrid success story, was developed at Cornell University in 1978, by crossing Macoun and an advanced (unnamed) breeding selection. As it matures, its green skin becomes a bright burgundy red, and the crunchy, crisp flesh develops a more pronounced flavor. Liberty's major contribution to the orchard is that it can be grown without the aid of fungicide or disease-controlling chemical sprays.

Two up-and-coming U.S. varieties originated as chance seedlings. Ginger Gold was discovered growing in Mountain Cove Orchards in Lovingston, Virginia, after surviving the widespread destruction of Hurricane Camille in 1969. Believed to be an offspring of Albemarle Pippin, Ginger Gold is named after Ginger Harvey, who owns the orchard with husband Clyde. A late-summer apple, Ginger Gold has greenish gold skin, pure white flesh and great flavor.

A more recent discovery is Cameo, which was found in the mid 1980s growing in an orchard in the foothills of Washington's Cascade Mountains. Cameo has cream-colored skin striped with red, and white-on-cream flesh that resists browning. These attractive qualities, along with its crisp texture and sweet-tart flesh, make it a desirable apple for salads and fresh desserts. Its supercrisp flesh holds up well in cooked and baked dishes, but it requires extra cooking time. Cameo was first made available to consumers in October 1998.

The Lore of the Heirlooms

One of the most promising trends in our ultra-modern times is the return of interest in heirlooms, in wonderful older varieties that got lost in the effort of mass production and distribution. (For information on specific heirloom varieties, see Hardy Antique Apple Varieties, page 176.)

More than 2,500 varieties of apples are grown at the New York State Agricultural Experiment Station in Geneva. One of the oldest agricultural research stations in the country, it is also the location for the United States Department of Agriculture's (U.S.D.A.) Plant Genetic Resources Unit, which houses the national apple collection. The apple varieties range from historical varieties that originated in Central Asia, to experimental hybrids from heirlooms that were brought as cuttings or trees to America by European and English settlers, to the antique apples of North America that were grown from seeds in the 18th century.

Many of these heirloom or antique apples rank among the best varieties for eating out of hand and for making the most flavorful pies, applesauce, and apple juice. However, because of their unreliable yields, susceptibility to diseases and misshapen fruits, few old varieties are grown in large commercial orchards.

In an effort to save important heirlooms that may contain unique genes, researchers at the Plant Genetic Resources Unit are always on the lookout for new genetic material. The reason has less to do with the fact that many of the heirlooms produce aromatic, intensely flavorful apples than with the fact that they represent genetic diversity. The key to safeguarding against the loss of genetic diversity is to rescue germ plasm, the genetic material contained in the seeds.

Seeds collected in Central Asia and planted in Geneva are now bearing fruits, ranging in color, form and shape from purple and cherrylike to yellow, conical, and of commercial size. The diversity of the wild and heirloom varieties growing at the Plant Genetic Resources Unit provides researchers with the opportunity to develop new hybrids and cultivars that will be disease and pest resistant, winter hardy, vigorous, and highly productive, and bear apples that are flavorful and firm.

Working with Heirlooms

While there is interest among apple growers in planting historical varieties on a commercial level, the economics discourage large-scale production. Even though heirloom varieties are available as dwarf and semidwarf trees, which bear quicker and more abundantly than their large spreading ancestors, they still take longer to bear fruit than the apple varieties favored by large commercial orchards.

The heirloom varieties are grown by a limited number of farms, such as Breezy Hill Orchard (profiled on page 150) in the Hudson Valley, New York, and Linden Vineyards in Linden, Virginia (profiled on page 83). To buy heirloom varieties from these orchards, and from other antique-apple growers around the United States, you must contact the orchards directly, or buy locally from specialty stores and farmers' markets. You'll also find farmers' markets and greenmarkets in major towns and big cities.

COOKING
with Apples

AS FAMOUS AS APPLES ARE FOR PIE, cooking with apples does not stop there. With even just a little imagination, you can use this versatile fruit in almost as many savory recipes as dessert dishes.

Cut into rings, apples can be sautéed along with pork chops and cider. Chopped and sautéed with onions, they elevate such pedestrian fare as braised cabbage and Polish sausage from Sunday's supper to a guest dish. When diced large, they make a delicious addition to any braised chicken recipe or pork and lamb stews. At some time or another, we've all had one of the many variations of apple stuffing with turkey and duck. Apple chutneys, relishes, and sauces may also take their place next to pork, poultry, goose, game, and curries.

For dessert, apples can be stuffed and baked, crisply frittered, folded into crêpes, mixed into cakes and breads, baked in tarts and pies, and hidden in cobblers, crisps, crunches, and brown Bettys.

Buying Apples

Apples are available all year round in North America. Obviously, weather and latitude play a big role in the distribution of apple orchards across the United States. Varieties that ripen in September in the southern states ripen around November in the north. Because of differences in the climates, an apple variety that tastes sweet and perfumed in Vermont may be flat and mealy in Virginia. In fact, in the north, some apples must be picked before they are mature in order to beat the first frost. Whatever the region, apples that are considered "best keepers" are left to ripen — often they become sweeter and more flavorful with age — in controlled-atmosphere storage at larger commercial orchards.

Unfortunately, after December, the apples that reach the consumers are often transported long distances, are left sitting around, and are not kept under refrigeration in the grocery stores or supermarkets. Some stores polish their apples to make them look even more appealing, and this removes the natural bloom. Once this bloom is removed, apples start to break down.

At the orchards, the loads of just-picked apples are so fresh and in such peak condition they haven't had time to bruise. It is for this reason that apple devotees go a little crazy every autumn. Starting as early as August sometimes and continuing through November, they make weekend pilgrimages to their local orchards and farm stands, looking for varieties that never reach the village markets or for those orchard jewels of limited production — such as Summer Rambo, Patricia, and Raritan.

Apple Grades

Although most apples are sold loose by the pound, quart, peck, or bushel, some retail stores sell them packaged in perforated plastic bags. The bags are stamped with the weight, variety, and U.S. grade — U.S. Extra Fancy, U.S. Fancy, with U.S. No. 1 meeting the minimum standards of quality.

Apples are graded mostly according to color and size. A very large, deep red Red Delicious will be Extra Fancy, while a small,

HOW MANY TO BUY

When buying just enough apples for a pie, 2½ pounds will do it — that's about five large, seven to eight medium, or nine to 10 small apples. A medium apple is approximately three inches in diameter.

A peck of apples weighs 10½ pounds, and there are 42 pounds in a bushel. It's cheaper to buy a bushel, but if you don't plan to go on an immediate cooking spree (this quantity would make about 16 pies or 20 quarts of applesauce), make sure you can store them until you're ready to use them, or that you have plenty of apple-loving friends.

somewhat greenish Red Delicious will be U.S. No. 1. I am frequently disappointed by large, perfect-looking apples. All too often they turn out to be tasteless and mealy.

Orchardists who sell locally grade their apples somewhat differently. Extra Fancy becomes Grade A, and Fancy is called Grade B, seconds, or "utility." Grade B apples grow on the inside of the tree and are not as colorful or as large, and sometimes they are not as sweet. Windfalls or bruised apples are also called "utility" or Grade 3.

Choosing Apples

There's nothing mystical about choosing apples. As a rule, what you see is what you get. If you bear the following points in mind, you'll end up with some pretty good specimens in your bag:

- Look for apples that are bruise free and firm to the touch. A bruise or blemish on the skin means a decay spot in the flesh.
- Overripe apples will feel soft, and the texture will be mealy or mushy. The background, or undercast, color will be a dull yellow or a dull green, instead of a soft light green or yellow.
- When the green of an apple is very dark, it is an indication that the apple is not fully mature. Such apples will be hard, will be sour, and will have poor flavor. Underripe apples are fine for cooking. If you want them for eating out of hand, refrigerate them and allow them to ripen slowly for a week or two.

Your decision to choose a particular variety should be influenced by what you plan to do with the apples. For the lunch box, you'll want crisp, crunchy, juicy apples. Summer apples that have these qualities include Ginger Gold, Raritan, Jonamac, Early Blaze, Patricia, and Paula Red. Later, I would choose Braeburn, Empire, Fuji, Jonagold, Macoun, McIntosh, and Mutsu/Crispin, among others. If you want to bake apples whole, or make pies, then choose those that hold their shape and retain their flavor, such as Northern Spy, Stayman, Jonathan, Jonagold, Braeburn, and others. (For a complete breakdown of best uses for apples, refer to the table on page 175.)

APPLE EQUIVALENTS

Size	Diameter in Inches	Sliced or Chopped	Grated	Finely Chopped	Sauce
Large	3¾	2 cups	1¼ cups	1½ cups	¾ cup
Medium	2¾	1⅓ cups	¾ cup	1 cup	½ cup
Small	2¼	¾ cup	½ cup	¾ cup	⅓ cup

To Peel or Not to Peel

There's a lot of goodness in the peel of an apple. It contains vitamin C, fiber, and much of the apple's flavor. So why not leave the skin on for all the recipes? Because some apples have tough skins; and even if the skin is not tough when the apple is eaten raw, it does not break down in the cooking process. Nothing, in my opinion, spoils a fine cake, pudding, or applesauce more than finding some cooked apple skin. You may leave the apple skins on in any of the recipes that call for peeling. Then see how you feel about "to peel or not to peel."

Planning to make gallons of applesauce? Then you may want to invest in a special strainer, available from specialty kitchen stores. For small batches of sauce, a Foley Food Mill does a fine job.

If a recipe calls for a lot of chopped or grated vegetables and apples, I use a food processor. When a recipe calls for cubed apples, I always prepare them by hand to make sure I get uniform pieces. A food processor will make very thin and very uniform apple *slices* in no time at all.

Storing Apples

Apples ripen 10 times faster in a dry, warm atmosphere than when they are in cold storage. Therefore, commercial orchardists store their apples in controlled-atmosphere (CA) sealed chambers. CA storage reduces (without arresting) an apple's intake of oxygen, which slows down its maturation process. This method prolongs the storage life of an apple by several months, and enables the orchardists to pick apples that are not meant for immediate consumption, before they are fully ripe. As they mature ever so slowly in CA storage, the good keepers retain their juicy, crisp texture while becoming more flavorful and sweeter.

The U.S. Apple Association advises consumers to refrigerate apples in the hydrator drawer, at temperatures anywhere from 32 to 40°F.

The best apples for keeping include Cortland, Delicious, Empire, Fuji, Granny Smith, Honeycrisp, Ida Red, Macoun, McIntosh, Mutsu/Crispin, Northern Spy, Rhode Island Greening, Rome Beauty, Stayman, and Winesap.

Summer apples harvested in July, August, and early September are not good keepers. These must be refrigerated immediately and used within four to six weeks. These include the following varieties: Ginger Gold, Jerseymac, Jonamac, Lodi, Patricia, Paula Red, Puritan, Raritan, Tydeman Red, and Wellington.

When keeping your apples under refrigeration, be sure to store them in perforated plastic bags or containers to prevent them from drying out.

With some varieties, even short exposure to warm temperatures causes over-ripening, a mealy texture, and loss of flavor. So whether you pick your own apples or buy them in a store, put them into a cool place without delay. However, check first for damaged or bruised apples and set those aside for immediate use. As we all know, a rotten apple in the barrel surely does spoil the whole crop.

Besides refrigeration, other methods of preserving a bounteous harvest include freezing and canning slices and sauce, and putting up preserves. See Preserving the Apple Harvest, pages 155–167, for more information.

Substituting Apples

I have given apple variety recommendations in most of the recipes in this cookbook, because some recipes work better with sweet apples, some with tart apples, and some with those apples that have a hard texture and don't fall apart. For example, in the Apple Puff Omelette on page 16, I have specified 2 large Cortland, Jonathan, or Ida Red apples. Any of these would be my first choice because of their flavor and texture. However, if these varieties were not available, I would choose another that had similar qualities. In this case, I would choose Granny Smith apples that were very light green, an indication that they were ripe and only mildly tart (as opposed to dark green and very tart) and because they have a firm texture. Failing that choice, I would then look for Golden Delicious, Jonathan, or Jonagold apples that were more green than yellow, an indication that they were barely ripe, having a firm texture and a more tart flavor than when completely yellow and fully ripe. If in doubt, refer to Meet the Apples: Apple Varieties, pages 168–180.

When a recipe calls for one large apple and yours look small to medium, substitute by the cup according to the table of Apple Equivalents on page 12.

Seasoning Without Salt

I grew up in a family where high blood pressure was a problem. For many years, salt was eliminated from our meals. This created no great exercise for my mother for the simple reason that the English like to keep their taste buds in shape by experiencing a variety of miniature taste explosions.

Our roast beef and ham sandwiches would be liberally smeared with eye-watering Colman's mustard. Thyme, sage, parsley, oregano, and garlic were kitchen staples that found their way into a great many stews and casseroles.

Apples and spices belong together. At times, I've had to restrain my urges to go hog-wild on these very fragrant powders. However, you may find that I haven't been generous enough for your taste in my recipes, so by all means experiment and add an extra pinch here and there.

So, although my mother uses salt judiciously today, I do not. However, you may want to add salt to taste in the savory dishes.

A GOOD BREAKFAST is touted as the best way to start your day; and what better way to add interest and nutrition to your breakfast than with apples? They go into everything from omelettes to pancakes, and they taste great alongside bacon, sausage, and ham. Apples add both flavor and moistness to a wide variety of breakfast breads, coffee cakes, and baked goods.

APPLE
Breakfasts & Breads

Apple Puff Omelette

This is a good way to make an omelette for four people so that everyone eats at the same time. You can prepare the apples the night before and heat them in a skillet for a couple of minutes the next morning. You can also keep canned apple slices in the pantry and substitute those in a pinch.

2 large apples (Cortland, Jonathan, Ida Red)

4 tablespoons butter

¼ cup brown sugar

1 teaspoon ground cinnamon

4 eggs

¼ cup granulated sugar

¼ teaspoon cream of tartar

1 tablespoon confectioners' sugar

1. Preheat oven to 450°F.

2. Peel, core, and thinly slice the apples.

3. Heat the butter in a medium-sized skillet, and sauté the apples for 5 minutes over low heat.

4. Mix the brown sugar and cinnamon. Sprinkle over the apples. Toss and continue to sauté the apples for about 10 minutes, until they caramelize. The mixture will be thick and syrupy.

5. Spoon the mixture into an 8-inch-square baking dish and keep hot in the oven.

6. Separate the eggs. Whisk the yolks and the granulated sugar in a small bowl until fairly thick.

7. In a large bowl, beat the egg whites with the cream of tartar until stiff and shiny. Fold into the yolk mixture, a third at a time.

8. Pour the egg mixture over the apples and bake for 8–10 minutes. The omelette will be puffed and golden. Remove from the oven and sprinkle with the confectioners' sugar. Serve immediately.

Yield: 4 servings

Sausage and Apple Omelette

I have made this omelette with soybean protein "crumbles" and also "veggie ground round." The flavorings and textures are uncannily sausagelike, making these foods good substitutions for the sausage.

4 ounces sausage meat

3 scallions, including green tops, sliced

1 medium apple (Granny Smith, Baldwin, Winesap, Empire)

½–1 tablespoon butter

4 eggs

freshly ground black pepper

1. In a medium-sized skillet, brown the sausage meat, breaking it up and turning it as it cooks, for about 8 minutes. Drain off most of the fat and push the meat to one side.

2. Add the scallions to the skillet and sauté for 2 minutes.

3. Peel, core, and chop the apple. Stir into the sausage meat and scallions and cook over low heat for 5 minutes. Remove from the heat and cover to keep warm.

4. Heat the butter in a medium-sized skillet over medium heat. Lightly beat the eggs and add to the foaming butter. Shake the pan to spread the eggs. As they set, use a fork to make a zigzag pattern from the edges to the center in several places. Shake the pan to keep the uncooked egg mixture moving.

5. After 2–3 minutes, the eggs should be set on the bottom, and the top should be creamy. Remove from the heat; spoon the sausage mixture onto one side of the eggs.

6. Fold the other half over the filling and slide the omelette onto a warm plate. Sprinkle with the pepper to taste. Serve immediately.

Yield: 2 servings

Apple Scramble

This is an easy way to have a good breakfast and satisfy a sweet tooth at the same time. It also makes a good after-school snack.

2 eggs
1 tablespoon honey
1 medium apple (Granny
    Smith, Braeburn, Empire)
1 teaspoon butter
1 teaspoon vegetable oil

1. Beat the eggs with the honey.

2. Grate the apple into the eggs. Stir to mix.

3. Heat the butter and oil in a skillet. When it starts to sizzle, pour in the egg mixture.

4. Start stirring immediately with a wooden spoon. Cook for 3–4 minutes, or until the eggs are cooked.

5. Serve on buttered toast for breakfast or a hot snack.

Yield: 2 servings

Apples for Breakfast and Snack Attacks

School-day mornings demand snack breakfasts that are nutritious and quick. These "recipes" make fast and easy breakfasts or an after-school snacks:

🍎 One-half-cup yogurt or low-fat cottage cheese topped with ½ cup applesauce and sprinkled with a favorite cereal.

🍎 1 cup yogurt combined with 2 tablespoons chopped walnuts, 2 tablespoons raisins, 1 small apple, chopped, topped with 1 tablespoon honey, and 1 tablespoon wheat germ.

🍎 1 apple, chopped and combined in a bowl with instant oatmeal and milk, as indicated on the packet. Microwave on HIGH as recommended, about 60 seconds. Drizzle with honey, spoon vanilla yogurt over the top and sprinkle with cinnamon.

🍎 2 slices of multigrain or whole-wheat bread spread with peanut butter and topped with thin slices of apple and slices of cheese; toasted in a toaster oven until the cheese begins to melt, about 2 minutes. Sandwich together if eating on the run.

Apple Frittata

*Truly, this is a great way to make a vegetable omelette pie.
In fact, a frittata may appear on my table for breakfast, lunch,
or even dinner. I may use leftover vegetables or a variety of fresh
vegetables in season. It tastes delicious warm or at room
temperature and is therefore excellent for a brunch buffet.*

1 tablespoon olive or canola oil

1 medium onion, chopped

1 red or green bell pepper, chopped

1 clove of garlic, minced

1 medium apple (Granny Smith, Empire, Braeburn)

4 eggs

2 tablespoons water

½ teaspoon dried sage

¼ teaspoon ground mace

⅛ teaspoon ground black pepper

½ cup grated Cheddar, Jack, or mozzarella cheese

1. Heat the oil in a medium-sized skillet. Add the onion, pepper, and garlic, and cook over low heat until the onion is tender, about 15 minutes.

2. Peel, core, and thinly slice the apple. Add to the vegetables and cook for 5 minutes.

3. Beat the eggs with the water, sage, mace, and pepper. Pour over the vegetables. Sprinkle with the Cheddar.

4. Cover the pan and cook over low heat for 10 minutes, until the eggs are set and the cheese has melted. Serve at once.

Yield: 2–4 servings

Breakfast Sausage Crêpes

This is one of my husband's favorite breakfasts. I make the crêpes (thin pancakes), and he cooks the sausages. You could also make the crêpes ahead of time and stack them between sheets of wax paper.

2 cups canned apple slices (page 157), drained

½ teaspoon ground cinnamon

½ teaspoon ground mace

3 tablespoons butter

8 link sausages, 5–6 inches long

8 crêpes (below)

maple syrup

1. Sprinkle the apple slices with the cinnamon and mace.

2. Heat the butter in a medium-sized skillet; sauté the apples for about 15 minutes, or until soft and golden. Keep warm.

3. Prick the sausages and cook over low heat in a greased skillet for about 10 minutes. Keep warm in a low oven or covered on top of the stove.

4. Roll the crêpes around the sausages, top with sautéed apples, and serve hot with maple syrup.

Yield: 4 servings

BASIC CRÊPES

This recipe is borrowed from the basic thin pancake recipe made with all milk. For thicker drop pancakes, use 1 cup of liquid to 1 cup of flour. If you are making dessert crêpes, add 2 tablespoons sugar and 1 teaspoon vanilla extract to the batter ingredients.

1 cup milk

1 cup sifted all-purpose flour

¼ cup water or apple juice

2 eggs

2 tablespoons vegetable oil or butter, melted

butter for frying

Apple Cheddar Crêpes

*You may want to use ready-grated mixed cheeses in this recipe.
Low-fat cheeses work fine, too; however, avoid the fat-free grated
cheeses — they have a rubbery texture when heated.*

3 cups canned apple slices
(page 157), drained

¼ cup apple juice or cider

1 teaspoon ground nutmeg

8 crêpes (below)

1 cup grated Cheddar or
Cheshire cheese

1 tablespoon butter, melted

1. Combine the apple slices, juice, and nutmeg in a medium-sized skillet, and simmer over low heat for 10–15 minutes, until the apples are tender and the liquid has almost evaporated.

2. Preheat oven to 375°F. Grease a shallow 9- by 13-inch baking dish.

3. Fill each crêpe with about ¼ cup of the apple mixture topped with 2 tablespoons or so of the Cheddar. (Spoon the filling onto the lower third and roll up from the bottom.)

4. Place the crêpes, seam side down, in the greased dish. Brush with a little melted butter and bake for 15 minutes, or until hot.

Yield: 4 servings

1. In a blender or mixing bowl, combine the milk, flour, water, eggs, and oil and beat until smooth.

2. Heat an 8-inch skillet over medium heat and add a small pat of butter.

3. Pour ¼ cup of the batter into the skillet and tilt until the batter covers the bottom. Cook for 1 minute or so, or until the crêpe is golden brown on the bottom. Turn with a spatula and cook for 1–2 minutes longer.

4. Repeat with the rest of the batter. Stack the crêpes between sheets of wax paper on a plate and keep warm in a low oven, or serve each one immediately.

Yield: 8–10 crêpes

Apple Pancakes

When I was growing up in Britain, pancakes were often served for dessert and without fail on Pancake or Shrove Tuesday. We squeezed fresh lemon juice over the pancakes and then sprinkled them with sugar.

2 cups sifted all-purpose flour

1½ teaspoons baking powder

1 teaspoon baking soda

1 teaspoon ground cinnamon

2 cups sour cream or 1½ cups plain yogurt

¼ cup apple juice or cider

¼ cup sugar or honey

¼ cup butter, melted

2 eggs

2 medium apples (McIntosh, Golden Delicious, Empire)

vegetable oil for frying

butter, lemon juice, sugar (optional)

1. Place the flour, baking powder, baking soda, and cinnamon in a large mixing bowl, blender, or food processor. Add the sour cream, apple juice, sugar, butter, and eggs. Beat or blend until smooth. The batter will be very thick. Allow the batter to rest for 30–60 minutes.

2. Core and grate the apples. Stir into the batter.

3. Heat a heavy skillet over medium-high heat and grease with approximately 1 teaspoon of vegetable oil. Drop the batter onto the hot griddle a few tablespoons at a time (for larger pancakes, measure ¼ cup batter).

4. When bubbles appear on top after approximately 2 minutes, turn and brown the other side. Serve with butter, lemon juice, and sugar.

Yield: 4–6 servings (16–20 pancakes)

PANCAKE GÂTEAU

Layer canned or cooked apple slices with a stack of pancakes to make a "gâteau," and drizzle the layers with melted preserves. To do this, make at least 6 thin 8- or 9-inch pancakes, cover one side with fruit spread, such as raspberry, apricot, or marmalade, and make layers with the apple slices in a baking dish. Bake at 350°F for 20 minutes, until hot. Serve drizzled with melted preserves and with a scoop of frozen vanilla yogurt or ice cream.

Apple Corn Hotcakes

Great for breakfast, these tasty, savory hotcakes also can replace bread or a side dish at dinner. The hotcakes are quite filling; often one or two per person will suffice. Leftover hotcakes can be crumbled and used as stuffing for Cornish game hens or chicken.

1   medium apple (Granny Smith, Ida Red, Golden Delicious)

1   tablespoon butter

1   scallion, thinly sliced

¾   cup yellow cornmeal

¼   cup sifted all-purpose flour

½   teaspoon baking powder

½   teaspoon baking soda

½   teaspoon ground mace

⅛   teaspoon cayenne pepper

¾   cup milk

½   cup grated Cheddar cheese

1   egg

vegetable oil for frying

1. Core and finely chop the apple.

2. Melt the butter in a skillet, and sauté the apple and scallion for 3 minutes.

3. In a large bowl, mix the cornmeal, flour, baking powder, baking soda, mace, and cayenne. Make a well in the center.

4. In a small bowl, beat the milk, Cheddar and egg. Add the sautéed apple and scallion. Stir into the cornmeal mixture.

5. Heat approximately 1 teaspoon vegetable oil on a griddle or in a heavy skillet over medium heat. When the oil is hot, drop ¼ cup batter onto the griddle and cook for 2 minutes or so, until the hotcakes are golden on the bottom. Turn and cook for 3 minutes longer. Serve immediately with butter, or keep warm in the oven.

Yield: 4–8 servings (8 hotcakes)

Grated-Apple Fritters

Fritters are a treat for any time of day, and they are a snap to make. To keep them crunchy, not soggy, cook them on high heat and don't overcrowd the skillet. Drizzle hot fritters with syrup or dust them with confectioners' sugar.

1 large apple (Rome Beauty, Fuji, Jonagold, Mutsu/Crispin)

2 eggs

½ cup sifted all-purpose flour

½ teaspoon baking powder

½ teaspoon baking soda

½ teaspoon ground cinnamon

½ teaspoon ground nutmeg

vegetable oil for deep frying

1. Peel, core, and grate the apple into a medium-sized bowl.

2. Separate the eggs. Drop the whites into a large bowl; the yolks into a small one. Whisk the yolks until light and stir into the grated apple. Add the flour, baking powder, baking soda, cinnamon, and nutmeg, and stir to combine.

3. Beat the egg whites until stiff and fold into the apple mixture.

4. Heat ¼ inch of vegetable oil in a hot skillet. Drop the batter by heaping tablespoons into the hot oil. Cook for about 1 minute, turn, and cook the other side for the same length of time. The fritters should be golden brown. Drain on absorbent paper and serve immediately, or keep warm in a low oven.

Yield: 2–4 servings (12–16 fritters)

Apple Ring Fritters

These apple ring fritters taste good at any time of day.
You don't have to let the batter rest for so long, but even
a short resting time seems to make the fritters puffier.

1½ cups sifted all-purpose flour
1 cup beer
1 tablespoon sugar
1 tablespoon vegetable oil
2 eggs, separated
5 large apples (Rome Beauty, Mutsu/Crispin)
2–4 cups vegetable oil for deep frying
confectioners' sugar

1. Combine 1¼ cups of the flour, the beer, sugar, vegetable oil, and egg yolks in a blender or food processor. Blend until smooth. Cover and leave at room temperature for at least 1 hour.

2. Core and cut the apples into ½-inch rings.

3. Pour at least 2 inches of oil into a wok or large skillet. Heat to 375°F.

4. In a large bowl, beat the egg whites until stiff. Stir the batter and fold in the egg whites.

5. Dip the apple rings first in the remaining ¼ cup flour to coat both sides, then in the batter. Fry a few at a time for 2–3 minutes on each side, until golden brown. Drain on absorbent paper.

6. Sprinkle with confectioners' sugar or serve with Apple Maple Sauce. (To make Apple Maple Sauce, blend 2 cups applesauce with ⅓ cup maple syrup and 1 teaspoon ground cinnamon or mixed spices.) Serve immediately.

Yield: 4–6 servings

Apple Doughnuts

If you have kids who like to help out in the kitchen, this is a good recipe to get them interested in bread making. Nothing beats eating bready little doughnuts you have made yourself.

2½ cups sifted all-purpose flour

1½ teaspoons baking powder

1 teaspoon baking soda

½ teaspoon ground cinnamon

½ cup sugar

3 tablespoons butter, softened

1 egg

¼ cup apple juice or cider

¼ cup milk

1 tablespoon vanilla extract

1 medium apple (McIntosh, Golden Delicious, Empire)

2–4 cups vegetable oil for deep frying

1. In a large bowl, combine the flour, baking powder, baking soda, and cinnamon. Make a well in the center.

2. In a small bowl, cream together the sugar and butter. Beat in the egg.

3. Add the apple juice, milk, and vanilla. Beat all together. Pour into the center of the dry ingredients and stir until smooth.

4. Peel, core, and finely chop the apple; stir into the batter.

5. Cover and chill the dough for 1 hour.

6. Place half of the dough on a floured board, knead lightly, and roll out to approximately ⅜-inch thick. Cut with a floured 2½-inch doughnut cutter.

7. Heat the oil to 375°F in a wok or skillet. Fry the dough for 1–2 minutes on each side, until golden brown. Do not overcrowd. Drain on absorbent paper.

Yield: 20 doughnuts

VARIATION

Doughnuts may be dusted while warm. Sift 1 cup sifted confectioners' sugar with 1 tablespoon ground cinnamon, and sprinkle over the doughnuts.

Girdle Scones

You can buy all kinds of flavored scones commercially today.
But they are so easy to make at home — my mother makes them
several times a week for family and company. Vary the flavors, if you
wish, by adding grated orange or lemon zest, or chopped crystallized
ginger. You can also add ½ cup chopped walnuts or raisins
without affecting the recipe.

¾ cup all-purpose flour

1 teaspoon baking powder

½ teaspoon baking soda

½ teaspoon ground cinnamon

½ teaspoon ground nutmeg

¾ cup whole-wheat flour

¼ cup sugar

4 tablespoons butter

1 egg

¼ cup plain yogurt or
   buttermilk

1 large apple (McIntosh,
   Golden Delicious)

1. Sift the all-purpose flour, baking powder, baking soda, cinnamon, and nutmeg into a large bowl. Add the whole-wheat flour and sugar and mix.

2. Cut in the butter with a pastry blender until the mixture resembles large crumbs. Make a well in the center.

3. Beat the egg and yogurt together in a small bowl.

4. Peel, core, and finely chop the apple. Stir into the yogurt mixture.

5. Pour the yogurt mixture into the center of the dry ingredients and, using a fork, stir to form a soft dough.

6. On a floured work surface, pat the dough into a ½-inch thick round and cut into 8 triangles.

7. Heat a "girdle" (as we call the griddle in Britain) or heavy skillet over low to medium heat and sprinkle lightly with flour. Cook the scone triangles for 5 minutes, until they are golden brown on the bottom. Turn and cook for 4 minutes longer.

8. Serve warm. Split and spread with butter.

Yield: 8 scones

Apple Coffee Cake

*This is a lovely company's-coming cake. You might
want to drizzle it with the Apple Glaze on page 124.*

3 medium apples (Golden Delicious, Gala, Braeburn, Empire)

juice of ½ lemon

1 teaspoon plus 1 tablespoon ground cinnamon

2 cups granulated sugar

1 cup (2 sticks) butter, softened

4 eggs

1 cup sour cream

1 tablespoon vanilla extract

2½ cups sifted all-purpose flour

1 teaspoon baking powder

1 teaspoon baking soda

½ cup brown sugar

1 cup chopped pecans

1. Preheat oven to 350°F. Grease and flour a 10-inch tube pan.

2. Peel, core, and chop the apples into small pieces. Place in a large bowl and toss with the lemon juice and 1 teaspoon of the cinnamon.

3. In a large mixing bowl, cream the sugar and butter until fluffy. Beat in the eggs, sour cream, and vanilla.

4. Sift together the flour, baking powder, and baking soda. Fold into the sour cream mixture.

5. Stir in the apples. Pour half of this batter into the prepared pan.

6. In a small bowl, mix the remaining 1 tablespoon cinnamon, brown sugar, and pecans. Sprinkle over the batter in the pan. Cover with the rest of the batter and smooth the top.

7. Bake for 1 hour 20 minutes, or until a skewer inserted into the cake comes out clean. Let cool in the pan for 10 minutes; turn out of pan onto a wire rack. Cool completely before cutting.

Yield: 15–20 servings

Apple Banana Bread

Like bananas, apples add moisture to cakes and breads.
The flavor here is classic banana, but you can spice it up by adding
½ teaspoon each of ground cinnamon and ground ginger.

1¾ cups sifted all-purpose flour

  2 teaspoons baking powder

  ½ teaspoon baking soda

2–3 ripe bananas, mashed (to make 1 cup)

  ½ cup brown sugar

  ⅓ cup vegetable oil

  2 eggs

  1 medium apple (Honeycrisp, Gala, Golden Delicious, Braeburn)

1. Preheat oven to 350°F. Grease and flour an 8- by 4-inch loaf pan.

2. In a large mixing bowl, combine the flour, baking powder, and baking soda. Make a well in the center.

3. Place the bananas in a medium-sized bowl. Beat in the sugar, oil, and eggs. Pour into the center of the dry ingredients and stir until just combined.

4. Peel, core, and dice the apple. Fold into the batter. Pour into the prepared pan.

5. Bake for about 1 hour, or until a skewer inserted into the center comes out clean. Let cool in the pan for 10 minutes; turn out of the pan onto a wire rack. Cool completely before cutting.

Yield: 12–16 slices

Louise Salinger's Apple Tea Bread

This is a lovely quick bread worthy of any afternoon tea, and because it freezes well, you can always have some on hand. Louise always uses apples from her family orchard; these days, she has more than ever to choose from, since her son, Bruce, has planted several of the modern hybrids. Some of the new favorites include Honeycrisp, Ginger Gold, Fuji, Braeburn, and Gala.

¾ cup sugar

4 tablespoons butter, softened

2 eggs

2 cups sifted all-purpose flour

1 teaspoon baking powder

1 teaspoon baking soda

2 large apples (Winesap, Fuji, Honeycrisp, Braeburn)

¾ cup chopped walnuts

1 tablespoon lemon juice

1 teaspoon grated lemon zest

1. Preheat oven to 350°F. Grease and flour an 8- by 4-inch loaf pan.

2. Cream the sugar and butter together in a large bowl.

3. Beat in the eggs.

4. Sift in the flour, baking powder, and baking soda. Stir to combine.

5. Core the apples and grate into the mixture.

6. Add the walnuts, lemon juice, and lemon zest. Mix thoroughly. Pour into the prepared pan.

7. Bake for 1 hour, or until a skewer inserted into the center comes out clean. Let cool in the pan for 10 minutes; turn out of the pan onto a wire rack. Cool completely before cutting.

8. Serve cold with a little butter on the slices. This bread freezes well.

Yield: 12–16 slices

Whole-Wheat Nut Quick Bread

This bread is packed with such nutritional goodness, eating a slice makes you feel as though you're doing your body a real favor. Eat it for breakfast, as a snack, or at lunch. For a dinner bread, substitute a mix of herbs such as basil, thyme, or oregano for the allspice.

2 cups whole-wheat flour

¼ cup bran flakes

¼ cup wheat germ

2 teaspoons ground allspice

2 teaspoons baking powder

1 teaspoon baking soda

¼ teaspoon ground cloves

½ cup apple juice or cider

½ cup applesauce

½ cup plain or vanilla yogurt

⅓ cup honey

⅓ cup vegetable oil

2 eggs

1 cup chopped walnuts

1. Preheat oven to 350°F. Grease and flour a 9- by 5-inch loaf pan.

2. In a large bowl, combine the flour, bran flakes, wheat germ, allspice, baking powder, baking soda, and cloves. Make a well in the center.

3. In a small bowl, mix together the apple juice, applesauce, yogurt, honey, oil, and eggs. Beat well and pour into the center of the dry ingredients. Stir to combine without overmixing.

4. Fold in the nuts and spoon the batter into the prepared pan.

5. Bake for 50–55 minutes, or until a skewer inserted into the center comes out clean. Let cool in the pan for 10 minutes; turn out of the pan onto a wire rack. Cool completely before cutting.

Yield: 12–15 slices

Barbara Mullin's Coffee Can Bread

I met Barbara many years ago, when she was working at Haight's Orchard in Croton Falls, New York. We used to trade recipes, and this is one of hers that I cherish. She would make up the breads as holiday gifts — such a nice idea that I have often done the same. The bread's round shape adds to its appeal.

4 medium apples (Cortland, Northern Spy, Winesap, Braeburn)

2 cups sugar

1 cup coarsely chopped pecans

3 cups sifted all-purpose flour

2 teaspoons baking soda

1 teaspoon ground cinnamon

½ teaspoon ground allspice

½ teaspoon ground nutmeg

1 cup (2 sticks) butter

1 tablespoon vanilla extract

2 eggs

1. Preheat oven to 325°F. Grease and flour three 1-pound coffee cans. Tie a double band of aluminum foil around the cans to extend 2 inches above the tops of the cans. Grease the insides of the foil.

2. Peel, core, and finely dice the apples. Place in a large bowl and mix with the sugar and pecans.

3. Sift in the flour, baking soda, cinnamon, allspice, and nutmeg. Mix well.

4. Melt the butter in a small saucepan and stir in the vanilla.

5. Lightly beat the eggs. Stir the eggs and butter into the apple mixture.

6. Spoon the batter into the cans.

7. Bake for 1 hour 15 minutes, or until a skewer inserted into the centers comes out clean. Let cool in the cans for 10 minutes; turn onto a wire rack. Cool completely before cutting.

Yield: 3 cakes, about 10 slices each

Bran Applesauce Muffins

*These are my weight-watching muffins. They have such
a good flavor, satisfy my sweet tooth, and make me feel
terribly virtuous. That is, if I eat only one at a time. And because
they go together so fast, I can mix and bake them first thing in
the morning and have one (or two) for breakfast.*

1 cup sifted all-purpose flour
1 cup bran flakes
½ cup whole-wheat flour
2 teaspoons baking powder
1 teaspoon baking soda
1 teaspoon ground cinnamon
½ teaspoon ground nutmeg
¼ teaspoon ground cloves
1 cup applesauce
⅓ cup vegetable oil
½ cup honey
2 eggs

1. Preheat oven to 400°F. Grease 12 large or 18 small muffin cups.

2. In a large bowl, stir together the flours, bran flakes, baking powder, baking soda, cinnamon, nutmeg, and cloves.

3. Make a well in the center of the dry ingredients and add the applesauce and oil.

4. In a small bowl, beat together the honey and eggs and add to the bran mixture.

5. Stir together until the dry ingredients are moist (a lumpy mixture makes tender muffins). Fill each muffin cup approximately two-thirds full.

6. Bake for 20–25 minutes, or until a skewer inserted into the center of a muffin comes out clean. Remove from the muffin cups immediately and cool on a wire rack or serve hot.

Yield: 12–18 muffins

Cornmeal Apple Cheese Muffins

I sometimes use a mix of grated cheeses, which may include Muenster and Cheddar. I do not use mozzarella or Swiss because of the texture. Over the years, I have switched from using cow's milk exclusively and now embrace low-fat milks made from soybeans and rice; they are also calcium-enriched and fortified with vitamins.

1½ cups sifted all-purpose flour

¾ cup yellow cornmeal

2 teaspoons baking powder

1 teaspoon baking soda

½ teaspoon ground cinnamon

½ teaspoon ground nutmeg

¾ cup milk (skim, low-fat, soy, or rice)

¼ cup apple juice or cider

⅓ cup honey

⅓ cup vegetable oil

2 eggs

¾ cup grated Cheddar cheese

1 medium apple (Granny Smith, Braeburn, Empire)

1. Preheat oven to 400°F. Grease 12 large or 18 small muffin cups.

2. In a large bowl, stir together the flour, cornmeal, baking powder, baking soda, cinnamon, and nutmeg.

3. In a small bowl, mix together the milk and apple juice.

4. Beat in the honey, oil, and eggs.

5. Make a well in the center of the dry ingredients and pour in the liquids and the Cheddar. Stir to barely combine the batter.

6. Peel, core, and finely dice the apple. Stir into the other ingredients until the batter is lumpy, not smooth.

7. Fill each muffin cup approximately two-thirds full. Bake for 25 minutes, or until a skewer inserted into the center of a muffin comes out clean. Remove from the muffin cups immediately and cool on a wire rack or serve hot.

Yield: 12–18 muffins

Honey Cream Cheese Spread

This is so simple, but it adds such a special touch to a breakfast table.

8 ounces cream cheese, softened

2–4 tablespoons honey

1 teaspoon grated orange or lemon zest

1. Combine all the ingredients. Beat well.

2. Use as a spread for muffins or slices of tea bread.

Yield: 1 cup

Apricot Cream Cheese Spread

You can make this easy spread with almost any favorite thick jam.

8 ounces cream cheese, softened

¼ cup apricot preserves

1. Combine the cream cheese and preserves. Beat well.

2. Spread on individual slices of quick bread, or use as a frosting.

Yield: 1¼ cups

Apple Date Spread

Naturally sweet and naturally good, this spread is delightful.

1 cup finely chopped pitted dates

½ cup apple juice or cider

8 ounces cream cheese, softened

1. In a small saucepan, simmer the dates in the apple juice, stirring, until the mixture thickens, about 5 minutes. Set aside to cool.

2. Beat the cream cheese until fluffy.

3. Beat the cooled date mixture into the cream cheese.

4. Chill and spread on individual slices of quick bread.

Yield: 1¾ cups

PICK YOUR OWN APPLES

Indeed, a wonderful way to celebrate the autumn harvest is to take friends and family on a picnic to a local orchard and spend the day picking your own apples. Some pick-your-own orchards also provide diversions that include warm apple cider and hot doughnuts, pumpkin patches, and hayrides. Most kids, however, find it a special enough experience to wander through avenues of trees and pluck apples right off the branches or find deliciously ripe ones that have fallen to the ground. Adults can take pleasure in discovering heirloom varieties that are not widely cultivated and rarely available except at the orchards and local farm stands or city-sponsored farmers' markets.

When you're picking apples in orchards that were planted decades ago, chances are the trees will be large, with the biggest and ripest apples growing on the highest branches in full sun. To help you reach those high-growing beauties, some orchards may provide ladders or telescopic picking poles with attached baskets. However, a quick shake of a nearby branch usually causes the tree to release apples that have reached perfect ripeness.

In more recently established orchards, most of the large, high-canopied apple trees of old have been replaced with high-yielding semidwarf and dwarf tree varieties, which bear an abundance of apples on branches that can be reached by adults of medium height.

When to Pick

While the main apple harvest falls between mid-October and November, some apple varieties, such as Jonagold, Stayman, Empire, Jonathan, and Golden and Red Delicious, are often ready for harvesting in northern states in late September or early October. Early October to Halloween is usually peak picking time for heirloom varieties such as Black Twig, Esopus Spitzenburg, and Ashmead Kernal.

Where to Pick

To find out where and when to visit pick-your-own orchards in your area, contact the county Agricultural Extension Office, Visitor and Tourist Center, or the local Chamber of Commerce. You'll also discover that some orchards host fall festivals. For Apple Picking Tips, see page 99.

"**AN APPLE A DAY KEEPS THE DOCTOR AWAY.**" So the old saying goes. If that's the case, you can feel healthy and food-smart whenever you snack on an apple or pour yourself a drink of cider or apple juice. If you are looking for something a little more elaborate, think of apple tea, punch, or wassail for a special drink. Substitute apple slices for crackers, bread, or chips. No matter how you serve them, apples are tasty and refreshing.

APPLE
Drinks & Snacks

Iced Apple Tea

I love green teas, particularly those flavored with honey, lemon, or mint. I choose basic, nonflavored green tea, however, when making iced tea because I'm going to add my own flavorings of honey, lemon, and mint. Adding the apple juice turns it into a drink that is reminiscent of the apple teas, both hot and cold, served in Turkey.

4 tea bags (green, orange pekoe, or herbal)

4 cups boiling water

1 tablespoon honey (optional)

2 cups chilled apple juice or cider

4 lemon slices

4 mint sprigs

1. Place the tea bags in a pitcher and cover with the boiling water.

2. Allow to steep for 5 minutes. Squeeze the tea bags gently and discard.

3. Stir in the honey, if desired, until dissolved.

4. Stir in the apple juice. Chill (or add a couple of ice cubes to each glass).

5. Pour into four tall glasses and drop a slice of lemon and a sprig of mint into each.

Yield: 4 servings

FREEZING CIDER

Cider freezes well. If you have space in your freezer, you might consider buying extra of your favorite cider in the fall to carry you through until the orchards reopen.

Frosty Apple Shake

*Make this with nonfrozen yogurt and you'll have a
delicious and healthful instant breakfast. I sometimes replace
one of the bananas with ½ cup applesauce.*

1 quart cold apple juice or
  cider

1 pint (2 cups) vanilla ice
  cream

3 ripe bananas

1 teaspoon ground cinnamon

1. In a blender, combine all ingredients, and blend until smooth.

2. Chill until serving time or use immediately.

Yield: 4 servings

Apple Smoothie

*When you want a really refreshing smoothie on
a hot summer's day, pop the applesauce in the freezer for
15–30 minutes before blending all the ingredients.*

2 cups applesauce

1 cup apple juice or cider

1 cup orange juice

2 tablespoons honey

½ teaspoon ground cinnamon

½ teaspoon ground nutmeg

1. Place all ingredients in a blender, and blend until smooth.

2. Serve immediately, or keep chilled until serving time. Sprinkle with additional cinnamon, if desired.

Yield: 2 servings

Fruit Crush

Can't be bothered to peel an apple or squeeze an orange? Then replace those ingredients with ½ cup applesauce and ½ cup orange juice.

½ cup sugar

½ cup water

1 cinnamon stick

4 whole cloves

1 orange

1 cup whole strawberries or melon balls

1 cup seedless grapes

1 large apple (Red Delicious, McIntosh)

1 lime

1 quart chilled apple juice or cider

1 bottle (7 ounces) club soda, chilled

1. Heat the sugar and water in a small saucepan over low heat. Cook, stirring, until the sugar dissolves, about 1 minute.

2. Add the cinnamon and cloves.

3. Using a small sharp knife, remove the orange zest — the thin outer orange peel — and add it to the syrup. Remove the syrup from the heat.

4. Cut the orange in half and squeeze the juice into the syrup.

5. Hull the strawberries, and slice them in half. Place them in a punch bowl.

6. Halve the grapes, and add them to the bowl.

7. Core and thinly slice the apple, and add it to the bowl.

8. Thinly slice the lime, and add it to the bowl.

9. Strain the syrup over the fruit.

10. Pour the apple juice and club soda over the fruit; stir and serve in glasses.

Yield: 4–6 servings

Apple Eggnog

To avoid the possible problem of salmonella, it's wise to avoid using raw eggs. The easiest way to do this is to use a pasteurized egg product.

½ cup pasteurized egg product (equivalent to 4 whole eggs)

½ cup sugar

1 cup brandy

⅓ cup rum

2 cups apple juice or cider

3 cups heavy cream

½ teaspoon ground nutmeg

1. Place the egg product in a large punch bowl and beat until frothy.

2. Add the sugar and beat until combined and frothy.

3. Beat in the brandy and rum, a little at a time, then the apple juice.

4. Continue beating and add 1 cup of the cream. Beat several minutes until the mixture thickens somewhat.

5. In a medium-sized bowl, beat the remaining 2 cups of heavy cream until almost stiff. Stir into the brandy and cream mixture.

6. Sprinkle the nutmeg over the top. Serve at once.

Yield: Approximately 18 servings

Wassail

*An old Twelfth Night tradition, this medieval drink of wassail
(from the Anglo-Saxon Wes hal, or "Be in good health," a salutation
offered when presenting a cup of wine to a guest) or "lamb's wool,"
as it is also known, is still served in some English homes around
Christmas. Some serve it with a spoon for eating the
baked apple that flavors the beverage.*

4	large apples (McIntosh)
¼	cup plus 2 tablespoons brown sugar
¼	cup apple juice or cider
3	bottles (12 ounces each) ale
1	cup sherry
1	cinnamon stick
½	teaspoon ground ginger
½	teaspoon ground nutmeg
	zest of 1 lemon

1. Preheat oven to 350°F.

2. Slit the skins of the apples horizontally about halfway down. Place in a greased baking dish and sprinkle with ¼ cup of the brown sugar and the apple juice. Bake, basting frequently for about 40 minutes, until apples are soft; remove from oven.

3. Pour the ale and sherry into a saucepan; add the 2 tablespoons brown sugar, cinnamon, ginger, nutmeg, and lemon zest; simmer for 5 minutes. Add the baked apples, stir thoroughly, and serve hot.

Yield: 4 servings

OPEN-FACE APPLE SANDWICHES

Forget the bread, crackers, and cookies — substitute apple rings instead. Topped with a variety of spreads, cheeses, and meats, they provide a welcome change on the hors d'oeuvre platter. They are particularly successful with children and health-conscious adults. Topping ideas are on the opposite page.

Wash and core the apples and cut into ¼-inch to ½-inch slices. Use Ginger Gold or Cameo apples, which are naturally slow to brown. Sprinkle the slices with lemon juice or drop them into a bowl of cold water with 2 tablespoons of lemon juice. Remove them; pat dry with paper towels.

Party Apple Punch

*Pineapples have long been a symbol of hospitality, and they
blend beautifully with apples in this refreshing punch.*

1 small pineapple or 2 cans
   (8 ounces each) unsweetened pineapple chunks
   or rings

2 apples (Red Delicious)

3 cups sparkling cider or
   sparkling white wine

2 cups apple juice

1 cup pineapple juice

½ cup brandy, applejack, or
   vodka

1. Cut the pineapple into ½-inch rings. Core, slice off the brown peel, and remove the eyes. Roughly chop the fruit and place it in a large pan. If you are using canned pineapple, drain the juice, reserving 1 cup for step 2.

2. Core the apples and cut them into ¼-inch slices. Add them to the pan along with the sparkling cider, apple juice, and pineapple juice.

3. Heat for 5 to 10 minutes, until steaming.

4. Remove the pan from the heat, and stir in the liquor.

5. Cool the mixture slightly, and pour it into a punch bowl or pitcher. Serve warm or cold, with or without the fruit.

Yield: 10 servings

APPLE-RING TOPPINGS

Depending on whether you are making snacks, lunch, or hors d'oeuvres, choose from the following toppings:

- Peanut butter and banana slices
- Peanut butter with raisins
- Peanut butter and applesauce
- Peanut butter and crumbled bacon
- Peanut butter and chopped nuts
- Cream cheese and chutney
- Cream cheese with onion slices and smoked salmon (or sardines)
- Cream cheese, cinnamon, and honey
- Cream cheese with diced ham, curry powder, and chutney
- Mashed blue cheese

Apple Cheese Spread

*I use low-fat cream cheese, because I find there is
little to distinguish its flavor from that of a whole-fat
version, but I use a rich, full-bodied Cheddar.*

8   ounces cream cheese, softened

1   cup grated Cheddar cheese, at
    room temperature

2   tablespoons brandy or sherry

1   medium tart apple (Granny Smith)

1   teaspoon dried basil

1   teaspoon dried oregano

1   teaspoon dried thyme

¼   teaspoon freshly ground black
    pepper

1. Combine the cream cheese, Cheddar, and brandy in a bowl. Beat until smooth.

2. Peel, core, and grate the apple; add it to the bowl.

3. Add the basil, oregano, thyme, and pepper; stir until thoroughly combined.

4. Spoon the mixture into a crock; cover and chill for approximately 1 hour. Serve on toast points or crackers.

Yield: 2½ cups

LOW-FAT OPTIONS

Just as low-fat cream cheese works well in the Apple Cheese Spread above, it can be substituted in recipes throughout this book. You may also use low-fat mayonnaise, milk, sour cream, and yogurt.

For a reduced-fat option, combine ingredients. For example, beat together half low-fat and half fat-free cream cheese or whole milk and skim milk.

HAVE AN APPLE, CHEESE, AND WINE PARTY

Many a time, the urge to throw a party has been squashed by the thought of all the preparation involved. One of the easiest ways to resolve this is to choose an apple, cheese, and wine theme. Accompany the apples, cheeses, and wines with an assortment of crusty breads, water biscuits, and crackers.

A visit to a local orchard, farmers' market, or the produce section of a large supermarket will allow you to procure a good selection of fresh, firm apples. Next, choose the cheeses and wines. Identify each apple variety and stack them in baskets next to those cheeses and wines that are considered complementary. Here's a list of apples, cheeses, and wines that go together well.

🍎 Golden Delicious or York. Serve with Edam, mild Cheddar, Camembert, and Brie cheese. Accompany by Medoc and Beaujolais red wines.

🍎 Jonathan or Braeburn. Serve with Scottish Dunlop (Cheddar), Gruyère, and Provolone cheese. Accompany by Bardolino and Valpolicella red wines, and Orvieto and Vouvray white wines.

🍎 Empire or Gala. Serve with Muenster, Fontina, and Bel Paese cheese. Accompany by Soave white and rosé wines.

🍎 Macoun or Honeycrisp. Serve with Caprice des Dieux, Excelsior, and Boursault cheese. Accompany by Moselle, Graves, Pouilly white wines, and Côte de Beaune red wines.

Apple Raisin Yogurt

Yogurt with fruit makes a great snack, breakfast, or dessert.

1 small sweet apple (Macoun, McIntosh, Gala, Honeycrisp)

1 cup yogurt (plain, vanilla, or lemon)

¼ cup granola

2 tablespoons raisins

1. Core the apple. Grate it into a small bowl.

2. Add the yogurt, granola, and raisins, and stir together. Chill, if desired.

Yield: 1 or 2 servings

Prosciutto Apple Wedges

A quick and delicious hors d'oeuvre, these wedges also make a wonderful and ever-so-easy first course. Depending on what follows, count on 2 to 3 wedges per person.

4 medium apples (Red Delicious, Cortland, Empire, Ida Red)

¼ cup lemon juice

4 ounces cream cheese, softened

½ pound prosciutto or smoked salmon

1. Slice each apple into 8 wedges.

2. Brush each cut surface with lemon juice.

3. Spread the cream cheese thinly on each cut side.

4. Wrap a thin slice of prosciutto around each wedge. Serve immediately or refrigerate, and remove from the refrigerator 30 minutes before serving time.

Yield: 32 wedges

APPLE THOUGHTS

"They [apples] must be eaten in the fields, when your system is all aglow with exercise, when the frosty weather nips your fingers, the wind rattles the bare boughs or rustles the few remaining leaves, and the jay is heard screaming around. What is sour in the house a bracing walk makes sweet."

— Henry David Thoreau, in his Journal

Hot Fruit

This makes a great snack or breakfast on a cold day. The grapefruit adds a pleasant tang to the mixture. Serve it by itself or spoon it over French toast, angel food cake, or a bowl of oatmeal or muesli.

1 large grapefruit, peeled and separated into segments with the skin removed from each segment, or 1 can (10 ounces or thereabouts) grapefruit segments

1 apple (Golden Delicious, Empire, Gala, Jonagold)

1 banana

¼ cup apple juice or cider

2 tablespoons raisins

1 tablespoon honey

1. Place the grapefruit segments in a medium-sized saucepan. (If you are using canned grapefruit, save the juice for another purpose.)

2. Core and chop the apple. Add to the grapefruit.

3. Peel the banana and cut into ½-inch slices. Mix with the fruit.

4. Add the apple juice, raisins, and honey to the pan and warm over low heat for about 10 minutes. The mixture should be hot enough to eat without scalding the mouth. Serve in bowls.

Yield: 2 servings

Apple and Sausage Bundles

This is my mother's adaptation of an Indonesian recipe that calls for chicken livers. We prefer the texture and flavor of the sausage, and we love the flavor and crunchy texture the apple gives to this recipe.

MARINADE

½ cup apple juice or cider

2 tablespoons creamy peanut butter

2 tablespoons soy sauce

½ teaspoon ground cinnamon

½ teaspoon ground ginger

SAUSAGE BUNDLES

4 sausages, each about 6 inches long

2 medium apples (McIntosh, Golden Delicious)

½ pound bacon

1. FOR THE MARINADE, blend together the apple juice, peanut butter, soy sauce, cinnamon, and ginger until smooth. Pour into a medium-sized bowl.

2. FOR THE SAUSAGE BUNDLES, cut the sausages into 1-inch pieces; add to the marinade, cover, and refrigerate. Marinate for about 4 hours.

3. Core the apples and cut them into the same number of slices as there are sausage pieces. (The slices should not be too thin, however.)

4. Drain the sausage pieces, reserving the marinade.

5. Cut the bacon strips in half crosswise. Make bundles by wrapping a strip of bacon around a slice of apple and a piece of sausage, secure with wooden toothpicks. Drop each bundle into the bowl to coat with the marinade.

6. Place the bacon bundles on a broiler rack and broil 4 inches from the heat. Broil them approximately 3 minutes per side, watching them carefully and turning them until the bacon is uniformly cooked and crispy.

Yield: Approximately 24 pieces (about 6 servings)

THE CRISP, CRUNCHY, TART, SWEET FLESH OF APPLES can be diced, sliced, or grated and added to just about any salad you may think of making. The understated flavor of apples lends itself to sweet and sour, creamy, garlic, herbed, and spiced dressings. So when you're short on lettuce, carrots, beets, celery, or any other salad ingredient, slice an apple into your bowl. Apples go into many savory side dishes; try mashed baked apples with creamed potatoes, turnips, carrots, and parsnips.

APPLE
Salads & Sides

Apple and Parmesan Curl Salad

I use a "gourmet" salad mix for this but, whenever I can, I harvest the tiny tender greens from my own garden. I also grow lots of arugula (rocket) and spinach, which I can grow and harvest for about 10 months in my Virginia climate.

½ cup olive oil

2 tablespoons seasoned rice vinegar, or balsamic vinegar

juice of ½ a lime or lemon

1–2 teaspoons Dijon mustard

1 clove of garlic, crushed

¼ teaspoon ground pepper

salt

1 pound baby salad greens or 1 packet ready-to-use baby spinach or salad mix

2 medium apples (Fuji, Gala, Golden Delicious, Ginger Gold)

½ cup pine nuts, toasted

4 ounces Parmesan cheese, shaved into curls

1. Combine the oil, vinegar, lime juice, mustard, garlic, pepper and salt to taste in a screw-top jar and shake well.

2. If using a head of lettuce, wash, dry, and tear into bite-sized pieces. Place the salad greens in a large serving bowl.

3. Core, halve, and slice the apples. Add them to the bowl.

4. Shake the vinaigrette again and add 1½ tablespoons to the bowl. (Serve the remaining dressing on the side.) Toss the salad, sprinkle with the pine nuts, and top with the Parmesan.

Yield: 4 servings

VARIATION

For a change, use crumbled feta or blue cheese instead of the Parmesan; toss with the salad greens and apple slices.

Spinach Apple Salad

If you can use homegrown spinach, it won't need as much washing and rinsing as loose store-bought bunches. However, if you don't grow your own, you have the option of buying a package of triple-washed spinach. There's nothing worse than crunching on gritty spinach leaves.

4   cups fresh spinach leaves

1   small head Boston or Bibb lettuce

2   medium apples (Cortland, Granny Smith, Golden Delicious, Braeburn)

¼   cup chopped walnuts

½   cup plain yogurt

1   tablespoon honey

⅛   teaspoon ground coriander

⅛   teaspoon ground ginger

⅛   teaspoon ground turmeric

1. Place the spinach and lettuce in a salad bowl.

2. Core and slice the apples. Add to the lettuce; toss in the walnuts.

3. In a small bowl, blend the yogurt, honey, coriander, ginger, and turmeric. Toss with the salad. Serve immediately.

Yield: 4 servings

Waldorf Salad

The absolute classic of apple salads, this traditional recipe is said to have originated at the Waldorf-Astoria hotel in New York City, during the early 1900s. The basic recipe lends itself to many variations — adding cubes of cooked meat, grilled fish, fresh mozzarella, or marinated tofu will turn it into a satisfying lunch.

3 medium apples (Jonagold, Cortland, Braeburn, Empire)

3 stalks of celery, diced

½ cup chopped walnuts

¾ cup heavy or whipping cream

2 tablespoons lemon juice

½ teaspoon ground white pepper

8 mint leaves or 2 tablespoons chopped fresh parsley

1 head Boston lettuce

1. Chill a medium-sized bowl for beating the cream.

2. Core and dice the apples. Place in a large bowl.

3. Add the celery and walnuts to the apples.

4. Beat the cream, lemon juice, and pepper in the chilled bowl.

5. When the cream is thick and stands in soft peaks, stir into the apple mixture.

6. Tear the mint leaves into small pieces and sprinkle on top.

7. Serve on the lettuce leaves.

Yield: 4 servings

KEEP 'EM WHITE

Tossing apples with vinaigrette, lemon juice, or syrup helps keep the flesh from browning. However, some of the up-and-coming apple varieties — particularly Ginger Gold and Cameo — have white flesh that is naturally slow to brown.

Stuffed Apple Salads

These make a lovely first course, so serve stuffed apples before the main dish. Or serve them for a light lunch with a choice of cheeses and a hearty whole-grain bread or corn muffins.

4 large apples (Cortland, Red Delicious, Mutsu/Crispin, Jonagold, Fuji)

½ lemon

2 medium carrots, grated

2 medium stalks of celery, chopped

1 scallion, including green top, chopped

¼ cup mayonnaise

¼ cup chopped walnuts

2 tablespoons sour cream

½ teaspoon ground nutmeg

⅛ teaspoon white pepper

1 head Boston lettuce

1 cup green seedless grapes (optional)

1. Core the apples. With a small paring knife, slice off the tops and remove the flesh, leaving ¼–½ inch of flesh on the bottoms and sides. Rub the tops with the lemon. Trim the blossom ends to make the apples sit level. Refrigerate.

2. Chop the removed apple flesh and place in a medium-sized bowl. Toss with the juice squeezed from the lemon.

3. Add the carrots, celery, scallion, mayonnaise, walnuts, sour cream, nutmeg, and pepper. Mix well. Refrigerate.

4. Arrange the nicest lettuce leaves on four plates. Place the hollowed apples in the center and fill with the chopped mixture. Sprinkle the grapes on and around the apples, if desired. Serve at once.

Yield: 4 servings

Apple Tortellini Salad

*For pasta salad lovers, this one from the Michigan
Apple Committee is hard to beat. Healthful, with low fat and
high fiber, it has lots of flavor, texture, and color. It makes a
wonderful addition to a party buffet.*

DRESSING

- 3 tablespoons frozen apple juice concentrate, thawed
- 3 tablespoons light corn syrup
- 2 teaspoons brown sugar
- 1 teaspoon apple cider vinegar
- ⅛ teaspoon garlic salt
  ground white pepper

TORTELLINI SALAD

- 1 package (9 ounces) refrigerated or frozen cheese-filled tortellini
- 3 medium apples (Empire, Fuji, Braeburn, Gala) cored and sliced (about 2 cups)
- 2 cups shredded salad greens
- 1 cup sliced fresh strawberries
- ½ cup thinly sliced celery
- ½ cup sliced scallions
- 2 tablespoons toasted pine nuts (optional)

1. FOR THE DRESSING, combine the apple juice concentrate, corn syrup, sugar, vinegar, garlic salt, and pepper to taste in a screw-top jar; shake well and refrigerate.

2. FOR THE TORTELLINI SALAD, cook the tortellini according to the package directions. Drain and cool under cold water. Shake gently to drain thoroughly.

3. In a large mixing bowl, combine the tortellini, apples, salad greens, strawberries, celery, and scallions.

4. Toss gently with the chilled dressing. Sprinkle with the pine nuts, if desired, and serve.

Yield: 8 servings

Potato Apple Salad

Fresh apples add a nice crunch to this potato salad, and they taste wonderful with the smoky-sweet bacon flavor.

6 medium potatoes

¼ pound bacon

1 medium onion

½ cup vegetable or olive oil

2 tablespoons cider vinegar

1 clove of garlic, crushed

2 medium apples (Cortland, Granny Smith, Jonagold, Fuji)

½ cup mayonnaise

1 tablespoon prepared mustard

1. Boil the potatoes in a covered saucepan for approximately 20 minutes, until they are tender but not falling apart. Peel while still warm and cut into ½-inch slices.

2. While the potatoes are cooling, fry the bacon, drain, and cut into ½-inch pieces.

3. Grate the onion into a large bowl.

4. In a small bowl, beat together the oil, vinegar, and garlic.

5. Add the sliced potatoes to the grated onion and, while still warm, toss with the oil mixture.

6. Core and dice the apples. Add to the potatoes. Add the bacon to the potatoes.

7. Mix the mayonnaise and mustard and spoon into the bowl. Toss to combine the mixture. Serve warm or chilled.

Yield: 4–6 servings

Curried Chicken Salad

Don't hesitate to substitute firm tofu for the chicken.
Do, however, use the type of tofu packaged in water; I would not
use silken firm or even silken extra-firm tofu in a dish that requires
tossing, because softer-textured tofu breaks apart too easily.

⅔ cup sour cream

⅓ cup mayonnaise

1 tablespoon honey

1 tablespoon lime juice

1 large clove of garlic,
   crushed

1½ teaspoons curry powder

½ teaspoon ground cumin

½ teaspoon ground ginger

2 apples (Granny Smith,
   Northern Spy, Winesap,
   Braeburn)

4 cups skinned, boned, and
   cubed cooked chicken

2 stalks of celery, diced

½ cup golden raisins

1 head Boston lettuce

1. In a medium-sized bowl, beat together the sour cream, mayonnaise, honey, and lime juice.

2. Add the garlic, curry powder, cumin, and ginger. Stir until thoroughly combined.

3. Core and dice the apples. Add to the mayonnaise, along with the chicken, celery, and raisins.

4. Arrange the lettuce on a serving platter. Spoon the salad onto the bed of lettuce.

Yield: 4–6 servings

Apple Slaw

I sometimes substitute chopped broccoli florets for the cabbage.
When I do this, I also chop the apples rather than slicing them.

2   medium carrots

1   medium red onion

4   cups thinly sliced or shred-
     ded red cabbage

2   large apples (Granny Smith,
     Fuji, Jonagold)

⅔   cup mayonnaise

⅔   cup sour cream

¼   cup ketchup

1   tablespoon lemon juice

½   teaspoon freshly ground
     black pepper

1   head Boston lettuce

1. Coarsely grate the carrots and onion into a large bowl. Add the cabbage.

2. Core and thinly slice the apples. Add to the cabbage mixture.

3. Beat the mayonnaise, sour cream, ketchup, lemon juice, and pepper. Mix into the slaw. Refrigerate for at least 1 hour.

4. Line a large bowl with the lettuce leaves and fill with the chilled apple slaw. Serve immediately.

Yield: 6 servings

ANTIOXIDANT POWERHOUSE

According to researchers, 100 grams of unpeeled fresh apple (about two-thirds of a medium apple) provides the antioxidant activity of 1,500 milligrams of vitamin C! Learn more about antioxidants and why apples are good for you in Apples for Good Health (page 183).

Unsweetened Applesauce

Unsweetened applesauce lends itself to any number of savory additions. For example, to serve it with beef, combine ½ cup freshly grated horseradish and 2 cups of applesauce. If pork or chicken is the main dish, add 2 tablespoons of honey, the grated zest of a lime and ½ teaspoon each of ground ginger and curry powder to 2 cups of applesauce. To accompany duck or goose, flavor 2 cups of applesauce with 2 tablespoons brandy and 2 tablespoons honey.

10 medium apples (any kind except Red Delicious or summer-harvested apples such as Lodi, Tydeman Red, Puritan; blending several types gives the best flavor)

1 tablespoon water, apple juice, or lemon juice

1 teaspoon ground nutmeg

1. Peel, core, and quarter the apples. Place in a large saucepan with the water and the nutmeg.

2. Cover the pot and simmer for approximately 30 minutes, or until the apples are tender. Mash with a fork or purée in a blender or food processor to the desired consistency.

Yield: About 5 cups

Note: For added flavor, leave the peel on and force the cooked apples through a sieve or food mill to separate the skins from the fruit. When puréeing in a blender or food processor, the skins will break down.

Apple and Sweet Potato Purée

*My favorite sweet potatoes have deep orange flesh. It's not
only that I find them more intensely flavored than the pale golden
sweet potatoes; I prefer their dense, smooth texture. While this purée
is a delicious side dish for savory meals, it also makes a good
base for a sweet or savory pie filling.*

2 large sweet potatoes

2 large apples (Rome Beauty, Northern Spy, Winesap)

4 tablespoons butter

¼–½ cup heavy cream or sour cream

½ teaspoon ground nutmeg

¼ teaspoon ground ginger

1. Preheat oven to 350°F.

2. Place the potatoes on a greased baking sheet and bake for 1½ hours, or until very tender.

3. Peel, core, and slice the apples.

4. Melt the butter in a skillet and cook the apples over low heat until tender, about 15 minutes. Transfer the apples to a large bowl.

5. Peel the potatoes while still hot. Add them to the apples. Add the cream, nutmeg, and ginger. Mash together with a fork, then whip the mixture with an electric mixer until the texture is creamy. Serve at once.

Yield: 6 servings

Chestnut-Apple Purée

Make this with canned chestnuts and purchased applesauce and you'll have a nice little purée ready in minutes. When making turkey or chicken sandwiches, instead of using mayonnaise, spread the bread (or flour tortillas) with 1 or 2 tablespoons of the purée.

8 ounces fresh chestnuts

2 cups unsweetened
    applesauce

½ teaspoon ground nutmeg

¼ teaspoon ground white
    pepper

1. Preheat oven to 400°F.

2. Cut an X into the flat side of the chestnuts. Place in a shallow baking pan and bake for 15 minutes. Stir occasionally.

3. Remove the chestnuts from the oven and cool slightly. Peel while still warm; otherwise, the brown inner skins will be difficult to remove.

4. Pass the peeled chestnuts through a ricer or use a blender or food processor to purée them. There will be approximately 1½ cups.

5. Pour into a 1½-quart baking dish and beat in the applesauce, nutmeg, and pepper.

6. Keep warm in a low oven until ready to serve.

Yield: 8 servings

Maple Sweet Potato Casserole

*While this dish is usually served alongside a savory entrée —
the sweet flavors are particularly fine accompaniments for roasted
meats and stuffing — it also makes a delicious warm or cold
sweet dessert served with whipped topping or sour cream
sweetened with brown sugar.*

6 medium sweet potatoes

2 medium apples (Baldwin, Granny Smith, Northern Spy)

  juice of 1 lemon

½ cup (1 stick) butter

½ cup pure maple syrup

½ teaspoon ground nutmeg

1. Scrub the potatoes and place in a pot of boiling water. Cook for 20 minutes, or until they can be easily pierced with a fork. Cool and peel.

2. Preheat oven to 350°F.

3. Cut the potatoes into ½-inch rings. Arrange a single layer of potatoes in a greased 9- by 13-inch baking pan.

4. Peel, core, and slice the apples about ½-inch thick. Toss with the lemon juice.

5. Place a single layer of apples over the potatoes. Continue layering until all the apple and potato slices have been used.

6. Melt the butter in a small saucepan. Stir in the maple syrup and nutmeg. Pour over the layers.

7. Bake for 30 minutes. Serve hot.

Yield: 8–10 servings

Apple Ratatouille

*I learned to make ratatouille when living as a student
in Geneva, Switzerland. My roommate would make a huge pot
and we would feast on it for days. Sometimes we had it over rice,
other times over noodles. When we were tired of eating it hot, we
layered it on thick slices of bread, sprinkled it with a little cheese,
and heated it in the oven. The apple in this version is an
interesting variation on the usual eggplant.*

2 tablespoons olive oil

1 large onion, sliced

4 cloves of garlic

2 teaspoons dried basil

1 teaspoon dried oregano

½ teaspoon ground allspice

¼ teaspoon freshly ground
    black pepper

2 green bell peppers, sliced

2 medium zucchini, sliced

6 ripe tomatoes, quartered

2 medium apples (Rome
    Beauty, Granny Smith,
    Northern Spy), diced

1. Heat the oil in a large skillet and add the onion. Crush the garlic directly into the skillet and sauté for 5 minutes.

2. Sprinkle the basil, oregano, allspice, and black pepper into the skillet.

3. Stir the bell peppers into the onions and sauté for 10 minutes.

4. Add the zucchini and the tomatoes to the skillet. Stir, cover, and simmer for 20 minutes.

5. Add the apples to the ratatouille, cover, and simmer for 15 minutes. Serve hot.

Yield: 8 servings

Rice-Stuffed Apples

Make a quick variation of this dish by using leftover cooked rice (jasmine is wonderful) and cooking the apples in the microwave on HIGH for 3–4 minutes per apple. Serve as a vegetable and grain side dish or a light lunch.

3 tablespoons butter

1 medium onion, chopped

1¼ cups water

½ cup uncooked rice

½ teaspoon ground allspice

½ teaspoon ground ginger

½ cup raisins

4 large apples (Rome Beauty, Mutsu/Crispin, Winesap)

¼ cup apple juice or cider

1. Preheat oven to 350°F.

2. Heat 2 tablespoons of the butter in a medium-sized skillet. Add the onion and sauté for 5 minutes.

3. Stir in the water, rice, allspice, and ginger. Bring to a boil, reduce the heat, and cover the skillet. Simmer for 20 minutes or until the rice is tender but not soft. Stir in the raisins.

4. Core the apples, leaving about ¼ inch of flesh at the bottoms. Scoop out approximately ¼ inch of flesh from the centers. Chop and add to the rice mixture.

5. Place the apples in a baking dish and spoon the rice stuffing into and on top of the apples. Add the apple juice to the dish.

6. Cut the remaining tablespoon of butter into small pieces and dot over the rice mixture. Cover the dish loosely with aluminum foil.

7. Bake for 45 minutes. Serve hot as a side dish with roast chicken or pork.

Yield: 4 servings

Apple Kabobs

*Stringing apple wedges on skewers makes them easy
to broil. They taste delicious with ham or chicken. Kabobs can
also be fun for a snack or dessert; drizzle them with a little
chocolate sauce for added sweetness.*

6 medium apples (Gala, Braeburn, Honeycrisp, Golden Delicious)

4 tablespoons butter

1 tablespoon smooth peanut butter

½ teaspoon ground cinnamon

½ teaspoon ground ginger

½ teaspoon ground nutmeg

1. Core and cut each of the apples into 6 wedges. Cut each wedge in half. Thread on six skewers and place on a broiling pan.

2. In a small skillet, melt the butter and stir in the peanut butter, cinnamon, ginger, and nutmeg.

3. Brush the apple chunks with the mixture and broil for 4 minutes (1 minute per side). Baste generously each time the skewers are given a quarter turn. Serve hot.

Yield: 6 servings

SPECIAL EQUIPMENT

If you're peeling, coring, and slicing apples in quantity, you may find it useful to acquire an apple peeler that also cores. I use a Colonial (old-fashioned) type of corer and a small paring knife to peel my apples, but there are also hand-cranked peelers that affix to the counter and electric appliances, often called strippers, that quickly peel apples.

Apple and Red Pepper Stuffing Balls

*Doesn't everybody love stuffing? Here is a novel way
to present it — not actually stuffed into the roast but baked
alongside in generous mounds.*

1 medium apple (Granny
   Smith, Braeburn, Ida Red)

2 tablespoons olive oil

2 red bell peppers, chopped

1 medium onion, chopped

1 clove of garlic, minced

6 slices whole-wheat bread

¼ cup apple juice or cider

1 teaspoon dried thyme

½ teaspoon ground mace

¼ teaspoon freshly ground
   black pepper

1 egg

1. Core and chop the apple.

2. Heat the oil in a large skillet and sauté the apple, bell peppers, onion, and garlic for 10 minutes. Remove from the heat.

3. Cube the bread and add to the skillet with the apple juice, thyme, mace, and black pepper.

4. Beat the egg and stir into the stuffing.

5. Form the stuffing into 4 balls and arrange around a pork or poultry roast for the last 45 minutes of roasting time.

Yield: 4 servings

Sausage and Apple Stuffing

Mild, sweet Italian sausages add good flavor to this stuffing. Simply skin them and crumble them into the skillet. You might also want to substitute sweet onions for the red ones.

½ pound pork sausage

1 medium apple (Ida Red, Empire, Golden Delicious, Granny Smith)

2 medium onions, chopped

½ teaspoon ground ginger

½ teaspoon ground mace

½ teaspoon dried sage

½ teaspoon dried thyme

¼ teaspoon freshly ground black pepper

8 slices whole-wheat bread

1 egg

1. Cook the sausage meat in a large skillet for 5 minutes, turning occasionally.

2. Peel, core, and chop the apple. Add the apple and onions to the meat with the ginger, mace, sage, thyme, and pepper. Sauté for 5 minutes.

3. Crumble the bread into the pan. In a small bowl, beat the egg, add it to the pan, and mix all together.

4. Stuff into a 10- to 12-pound turkey and bake. The stuffing can be baked separately in a greased 1½-quart baking dish for 45 minutes at 350°F.

Yield: Stuffing for a 10- to 12-pound turkey

ADD AN APPLE

Among my favorite apple side dishes are apple-based stuffings. An apple can be added to almost any stuffing recipe without throwing it off balance; it will impart only a mild flavor, but it will make the stuffing a little more moist. Use ¼ cup apple juice to replace some water or broth in your stuffing — it will make the dressing a touch sweeter.

Corn Bread Apple Stuffing

Make your own corn bread or muffins from scratch (or from a mix) the day before so you can enjoy them fresh for dinner; then use the leftovers in the stuffing the following day.

2–4 tablespoons olive oil or butter

2 medium stalks of celery, chopped

1 medium onion, chopped

¼ cup chopped fresh parsley

1 teaspoon dried oregano

2 medium apples (Empire, Ida Red, Golden Delicious)

2 cups crumbled corn bread (2 large muffins or 4 slices of bread)

2 tablespoons apple juice

1 egg

1. Heat the oil in a skillet and sauté the celery and onion for 5 minutes. Add the parsley and oregano.

2. Peel, core, and chop the apples. Sauté with the onion mixture for 5 minutes.

3. Stir in the corn bread.

4. Beat together the apple juice and egg. Mix into the stuffing.

5. Stuff into a 5- to 6-pound chicken and bake. The stuffing can be baked separately in a greased 1-quart baking dish for 45 minutes at 350°F.

Yield: Stuffing for a 5- to 6-pound chicken

Marla Rathbun's Onion Apple Stuffing

*Marla is an old friend who lives in Poughkeepsie,
New York. Not only is she a great cook, she is a professional
violinist and music teacher. Although she usually uses this stuffing
for turkey, it goes very well with a chicken or a goose.*

½ cup (1 stick) butter

18 medium onions, sliced

5 stalks of celery, sliced

4 cups bread cubes (8 slices of bread)

¼ cup chopped fresh parsley

1 tablespoon chopped fresh sage

1 tablespoon fresh thyme

½ teaspoon freshly ground black pepper

4 large apples (Ida Red)

1. In a large skillet, melt ¼ cup of the butter. Add the onions and cook over low heat for about 20 minutes, or until softened and light golden. Set aside.

2. In a second skillet, melt the remaining ¼ cup butter and sauté the celery for 5 minutes.

3. Toss in the bread cubes, parsley, sage, thyme, and, and pepper.

4. Peel, core, and dice the apples; stir them into the bread mixture.

5. Stir the onions into the stuffing. Stuff into two 6- to 8-pound geese or one 12- to 14-pound turkey. Excess stuffing can be baked separately in a greased 2-quart baking dish for 45 minutes at 350°F.

Yield: Stuffing for two 6–8-pound geese or one 12–14-pound turkey

Spicy Cranberry Apple Relish

This can also be turned into a salsa to serve with turkey-stuffed flour tortillas. Spice it up by adding extra chopped onion and a minced jalapeño or other hot pepper.

2 apples (Granny Smith, Empire, Braeburn)

1 orange

½ cup sugar

2 cups cranberries

1 small onion

2 tablespoons lemon juice

¼ teaspoon cayenne pepper

¼ teaspoon ground cloves

1 tablespoon brandy

1 teaspoon ground ginger

1. Core and cut each of the apples into about 8 pieces. Process in a food processor until coarsely chopped. Transfer to a medium-sized bowl.

2. Remove the orange zest in thin strips, being careful not to include the white pith. Process the zest with the sugar in a food processor until finely chopped. Transfer to the bowl. Squeeze in the orange juice.

3. Process the cranberries, 1 cup at a time, until coarsely chopped. Add to the apples and orange zest.

4. Peel and cut the onion into 4 pieces. Process until coarsely chopped. Add with the lemon juice, cayenne, cloves, brandy, and ginger to the bowl and stir.

5. Cover the bowl and refrigerate for a day or two before serving.

Yield: 4 cups

Fall Fruit Relish

Tart cranberries are mellowed with the natural sweetness of apples and pears for a fine condiment for roasts or poultry. If you prefer an even sweeter relish, dissolve 2 tablespoons honey or pure maple syrup in the apple juice.

2 sweet apples (Golden Delicious, Gala, Honeycrisp), cored and finely chopped

2 medium pears, peeled, cored and chopped

¾ cup cranberries, coarsely chopped

½ cup chopped pitted dates

½ cup chopped walnuts or pecans, toasted

½ cup apple juice

1 teaspoon grated orange zest

¼–½ teaspoon ground cinnamon

⅛ teaspoon ground cloves

1. Combine all ingredients and refrigerate. To save leftover relish, place in a covered jar and refrigerate for up to 2 weeks.

Yield: 4 cups

TOP 10 GROWN IN THE UNITED STATES

Although more than 2,500 varieties of apples are grown in the United States, only 100 varieties are grown commercially, with 15 of them accounting for more than 90 percent of the annual production. The U.S. Apple Association reported the following statistics for estimated 2000 U.S. production:

VARIETY	BUSHELS (42 POUNDS EACH)
1. Red Delicious	89,299,000
2. Golden Delicious	35,387,000
3. Fuji	20,346,000
4. Granny Smith	19,647,000
5. Gala	16,154,000
6. Rome Beauty	13,097,000
7. McIntosh	11,247,000
8. Jonathan	5,302,000
9. York	4,633,000
10. Empire	4,290,000

APPLESAUCE IN MEAT LOAF. Of course, it makes a very moist and tasty one. Grated, sliced, or cubed, apples add another dimension to soups, meat pies, poultry, pork, beef, and lamb. In fact, is there any meat dish that can't take apples? Whether you are preparing a casual supper or a formal dinner, apples belong on the menu.

APPLES
Make the Meal

Mulligatawny Soup

A delicious soup that my mother made whenever she had leftover chicken and rice, mulligatawny, meaning "pepper water," originated in India. It was popularized in the British Isles by English and Scottish soldiers and their returning descendants.

2 tablespoons olive oil or butter

1 medium carrot, chopped

1 medium onion, chopped

1 small stalk of celery, chopped

1 medium apple (Granny Smith, Newtown Pippin, Braeburn, Stayman)

2 tablespoons all-purpose flour

3 teaspoons curry powder

5 cups chicken or vegetable stock

1 cup cooked rice

½ cup heavy or light cream

1. Heat the oil in a 3-quart saucepan and sauté the carrot, onion, and celery for 5 minutes.

2. Peel, core, and dice the apple. Stir into the vegetables and sauté for 5 minutes.

3. Stir in the flour and curry powder.

4. Gradually pour in the stock and bring to a boil. Reduce the heat, cover the pan, and simmer for 20 minutes.

5. Add the rice and simmer for 10 minutes longer. Remove from the heat.

6. To scald the cream, heat it in a small saucepan to just below boiling (tiny bubbles will form at the edge of the liquid). Add to the soup and serve.

Yield: 4–6 servings

Zucchini and Apple Soup

Whether served hot or at room temperature, this starter goes together very fast and can be made while the rest of the dinner is cooking. Or serve it at lunch accompanied by crusty bread and an olive tapenade.

1 large apple (Rome Beauty, Northern Spy, Winesap)

2 tablespoons butter

1 tablespoon olive oil

2 medium zucchini, chopped

1 large onion, sliced

½ cup cider or sherry

½ teaspoon ground nutmeg

½ teaspoon freshly ground black pepper

4 cups chicken or vegetable stock

½ cup light cream

½ cup chopped fresh parsley

ground nutmeg (optional)

1. Peel, core, and dice the apple.

2. Heat the butter and oil in a large skillet. Add the apple, zucchini, and onion; sauté over medium heat for 5–10 minutes, until soft.

3. Add the cider, nutmeg, and pepper. Cover the pan and simmer 15 minutes longer.

4. Add the stock, cover the pan, and simmer for 5 minutes.

5. Purée the vegetables in a blender or food processor (or force through a sieve).

6. Return the vegetables to the skillet, add the cream, and bring to a fast boil.

7. Pour into serving bowls and sprinkle with the parsley; dust with additional pepper, and a little ground nutmeg, if desired.

Yield: 4–6 servings

Black Bean Soup

Make this with canned beans, rinsed to remove the salt, and cut your preparation time down to 15 minutes and the cooking time to 30 minutes. Serve the soup over brown or white rice for a heartier meal.

1 pound dried black beans (turtle beans)

6 cups water

2 tablespoons olive oil

4 large cloves of garlic, chopped

2 large stalks of celery, chopped

1 large onion, chopped

3½ cups beef, chicken, or vegetable stock

½ cup sherry

2 teaspoons ground allspice

1 bay leaf

2 tart apples (Granny Smith, Jonagold, Winesap, Ida Red)

½ pound sweet Italian sausage links, cut into 2-inch pieces

½ pound hot Italian sausage links, cut into 2-inch pieces

1. Wash and pick over the beans. Place in a large pot, add the water, and heat to boiling. Remove from the heat, cover the pot, and set aside to soak for 1 hour.

2. Heat the oil in a 4- to 5-quart Dutch oven, and sauté the garlic, celery, and onion for 5 minutes.

3. Add the stock, sherry, allspice, and bay leaf. Drain the beans and add to the Dutch oven. Bring to a boil, reduce the heat, and simmer for 2–4 hours (depending on how tender you like the beans).

4. Peel, core, and dice the apples. Add with the sausage to the beans during the last 30 minutes of cooking.

Yield: 6–8 servings

Apple Rarebit Supper

*A takeoff on Welsh Rarebit, which is often made with
beer and rarely with apples. My mother used to serve rarebit
regularly for a school-day breakfast or a Saturday high tea.
She, however, made ours with milk, never beer.*

¾ pound Cheddar cheese

1 tablespoon butter

1 large apple (Rome Beauty,
   Winesap, Fuji)

½ cup heavy or light cream

1 teaspoon dry mustard

½ teaspoon ground nutmeg

4 slices bread, toasted

1. Grate the Cheddar into a medium-sized saucepan. Add the butter.

2. Grate the apple into the pan. Add the cream, mustard, and nutmeg.

3. Cook over low heat, stirring, until all ingredients are blended.

4. When the mixture begins to bubble, pour over buttered toast and serve.

Yield: 4 servings

FIVE A DAY

The medical profession recommends that we eat five to seven servings of fruits and vegetables each day. But what is a serving? Each of the following apple measurements can be counted as one daily serving of fruit:

- one medium apple
- 8 ounces of 100-percent pure apple juice (not "cocktail" juice, juice "beverages," or "drinks," which are often diluted and contain sugar or syrup)
- ½ cup of applesauce
- For the Nutrition Facts labeling purposes, the Food and Drug Administration (F.D.A.) defines a serving size of juice as 8 ounces. The American Dietetic Association defines a serving size of juice as 6 ounces.

Baked Apples and Cheese

What a wonderful combination — freshly grated
Cheddar cheese and apples, good enough to eat between two
pieces of whole-grain bread. The leeks add a winning quality to
this custard dish. Served hot, warm, or cold, it's a good choice
for a light main meal or for a brunch buffet.

1 large leek

2 tablespoons butter

3 cups canned apple slices (page 157), drained

1 cup grated Cheddar cheese

1½ cups half-and-half or light cream

3 eggs

1 teaspoon ground nutmeg

¼ teaspoon freshly ground black pepper

1. Preheat oven to 350°F.

2. Wash the leek and discard the outer layer and any of the tougher green leaves. Cut into ¼-inch rings.

3. Heat the butter in a skillet, add the leek, and sauté for 5 minutes. Put into an 8-inch-square baking dish.

4. Layer the apple slices on top and sprinkle with the Cheddar.

5. Beat the half-and-half, eggs, nutmeg, and pepper. Pour over the Cheddar.

6. Bake for 40–45 minutes, until the custard is set and a knife inserted into the center comes out clean.

Yield: 6 servings

Grilled Tuna with Apple Chutney

*My friend Ivan Lillie, a caterer and private chef,
has served me some pretty wonderful meals. Of the many recipes
I've borrowed from him, this is one of my favorites.*

8 tuna steaks, cut 1-inch thick

½ cup apple cider vinegar

½ cup seasoned rice wine vinegar

6 large chunks crystallized ginger, chopped

4 cloves of garlic, minced

1 tablespoon brown sugar

 salt and freshly ground black pepper

2 tablespoons olive oil

1 tablespoon sesame oil

APPLE CHUTNEY

2 jalapeño peppers

4 apples (Ida Red, York, Stayman, Braeburn), peeled, cored, and diced

1 medium white onion, diced

6–8 cloves of garlic, chopped

½ cup apple cider vinegar

½ cup brown sugar

1. Place the tuna steaks in a large dish. For the marinade, combine the cider vinegar, rice wine vinegar, ginger, garlic, sugar, and salt and pepper to taste, and stir well. Pour the marinade over the tuna and leave at room temperature for about 30 minutes, turning the tuna in the marinade once or twice.

2. TO MAKE THE CHUTNEY, wear rubber gloves to seed and mince the peppers. Combine the peppers, apples, onion, garlic, vinegar, and sugar in a medium-sized saucepan; simmer over low heat for about 20 minutes, stirring occasionally, until the apples are tender.

3. Remove the tuna from the dish; pour off and discard the marinade. Return the tuna to the dish. In a small bowl, combine the olive and sesame oils; drizzle over the tuna. Turn the steaks to oil both sides.

4. Heat the grill to high, and position the racks 4 inches from the heat. Grill the tuna steaks for 2–3 minutes on each side for rare (3–4 minutes for medium rare).

5. Serve each tuna steak with a generous spoonful of the chutney.

Yield: 8 servings

Tuna Apple Tortilla Wraps

*I often make a wrap for a quick and easy lunch.
The flour tortillas are lighter than the two slices of bread
I'd use to make a sandwich and the filling is lean and healthful.*

2 8-inch flour tortillas

2 tablespoons spread, such
as herbed cream cheese,
puréed roasted peppers,
hummus, or baba
ghanoush

1 large apple (Nittany, Gala,
Braeburn, Golden
Delicious), washed, cored,
and thinly sliced

1 can (6½ ounces) solid white
tuna in water, drained

½–1 tablespoon reduced-fat
mayonnaise or sour
cream

freshly ground black
pepper

mild curry powder
(optional)

2 scallions with green tops,
cut in half and sliced in
half lengthwise

1. Place the tortillas on dinner plates and spread each with 1 tablespoon of the spread of your choice.

2. Arrange apple slices down the center of the tortillas, staying well within 1 inch from the front and back edges.

3. In a small bowl, flake the tuna and combine with the mayonnaise and pepper to taste.

4. Spoon the tuna mixture over the apple slices. Sprinkle with a dash of mild curry powder, if desired. Top with the scallions.

5. Roll the wraps from front to back and serve immediately. To take along in a lunch box or brown bag, wrap securely in plastic wrap or place in a resealable plastic bag.

Yield: 2 wraps

VARIATION:

You may also fill the wraps with leftover grilled fresh tuna or salmon, turkey or chicken breast, or smoked salmon. The flavor of apple also goes well with the fresh buffalo mozzarella I buy from a dairy just outside Leesburg, Virginia.

Codfish and Apple Curry

The large, solid flakes of cod make it an ideal choice for this dish. However, you may want to substitute scallops, shrimp, monkfish, or even surimi crab. I usually use a mild curry for this dish, but there's no reason not to use a spicy one if that is more to your taste.

1 tablespoon olive oil

1 large onion, chopped

2 cloves of garlic, minced

1 can (28 ounces) crushed tomatoes

¼ cup raisins

2 tablespoons chutney

2 teaspoons curry powder (or to taste)

2 medium apples (Golden Delicious, Empire, Honeycrisp, Ginger Gold)

1½ pounds cod steaks

1. Heat the oil in a large skillet and sauté the onion and garlic for 10 minutes.

2. Add the tomatoes, raisins, chutney, and curry powder to the skillet.

3. Peel, core, and chop the apples. Stir into the simmering mixture. Cook for 15–20 minutes, until the onions and apples are tender.

4. Remove the skin and bones, if necessary, from the cod, and cut into bite-size pieces. Stir into the curry and cook for 5–10 minutes or just until tender. Serve over rice, if desired.

Yield: 4 servings

Chicken with Sour Cream

*An easy dinner to prepare for family or for company.
Serve this with rice, couscous, or egg noodles. Reheat leftover
chicken in a pan on top of the stove and simmer gently.*

2 tablespoons olive oil

1 large onion, chopped

2 medium stalks of celery, chopped

2–4 cloves of garlic, minced

1 4-pound chicken, cut into serving pieces

1 teaspoon ground cumin

½ teaspoon ground cinnamon

½ teaspoon ground ginger

¼ teaspoon freshly ground black pepper

1 cup white wine or chicken stock

1 cup tomato juice

2 tablespoons cornstarch

1 tablespoon honey

2 apples (Golden Delicious)

1 cup sour cream at room temperature

1. Preheat oven to 350°F.

2. Heat the oil in a 5- to 6-quart Dutch oven and sauté the onion, celery, and garlic over medium heat.

3. Remove the skin from the chicken and lay the pieces on top of the sautéed vegetables in the Dutch oven. Add the giblets and liver if desired.

4. Sprinkle with the cumin, cinnamon, ginger, and pepper.

5. Cover with the wine and tomato juice, reserving a little of the liquid to mix with the cornstarch. Make a paste with the cornstarch and reserved liquid.

6. Bring the liquids in the Dutch oven to a boil, reduce the heat to low, and stir in the cornstarch paste and the honey.

7. Cover the pot and place in the oven for 45 minutes, or until the chicken is nearly tender.

8. Peel, core, and cube the apples. Remove the pot from the oven; stir the apples and sour cream into the Dutch oven. Return to the oven and cook for 15–20 minutes longer. Serve at once.

Yield: 4 servings

Cider-Braised Chicken

You can also make this in a slow cooker. Prepare as recommended without adding the cornstarch and set the cooker to low heat for 7–9 hours or high heat for 3–4 hours. Add the cornstarch at the end of the cooking and cook on high heat for about 15 minutes longer to thicken the liquids.

1   4-pound chicken, cut into quarters

1   tablespoon ground turmeric

1   teaspoon ground ginger

½   teaspoon ground mace

¼   teaspoon ground allspice

4   tomatoes, quartered

1   cup apple juice or cider

1   tablespoon cornstarch

2   tablespoons cold water

1. Remove the wing tips, backbone, and parson's nose (stubby tailpiece) from the chicken pieces; freeze for making stock. Discard any fat.

2. Brown the chicken in a large skillet over medium heat (do not use oil), skin-side down, for about 10 minutes. Pour off excess fat.

3. Sprinkle with the turmeric, ginger, mace, and allspice; add the tomatoes. Cover with the apple juice.

4. Cover the pan, reduce the heat, and simmer for 45 minutes.

5. To thicken the juices, make a paste by combining the cornstarch with the water. Stir into the juices and simmer, uncovered, for 15 minutes longer.

Yield: 4 servings

Roast Chicken with Apples, Turnips, and Garlic

This recipe is from Jim Law of Linden Vineyards, antique-apple growers in Linden, Virginia. Occasionally, Linden hosts "apple dinners" during the fall, and this, he says, is a proven favorite. He recommends using aromatic Ashmead Kernels, but don't hesitate to substitute Jonathan, Jonagold, Braeburn, or other crunchy, flavorful apples.

1   tablespoon paprika

½   teaspooon freshly ground black pepper

½   teaspoon salt

1   3-pound chicken

3   medium apples (Ashmead Kernels), cored, peeled (if desired), and cut into eighths

3   small white turnips, peeled, quartered, and thinly sliced

6   cloves of garlic, peeled

juice of half a lemon

1. Preheat oven to 350°F.

2. Combine the paprika, pepper, and salt and rub the chicken inside and out with the mixture.

3. Lightly oil or spray a roasting pan, add the chicken, breast side up, and arrange the apples, turnips, and garlic around the sides. Trickle the lemon juice over the apples and turnips.

4. Roast the chicken until it is golden brown all over, about 1 hour 15 minutes. Baste with pan juices two or three times during the roasting.

5. When the chicken is done, remove it to a serving platter and spoon the apples, turnips, and garlic into a food processor. Skim the fat from the pan and pour the remaining juice over the vegetables. Process to a purée consistency and serve separately with the chicken.

Yield: 4–6 servings

Linden Vineyards

Owner: Jim Law

At his Virginia orchard, Jim Law grows 300 trees of each of six heirloom varieties. "We have limited varieties because we have taken out some that didn't do well for us," said Law. "For a few years we grew two of the modern hybrids — Scarlet Gala and Jonagold — but it was not a direction we wanted to go, so we pulled them out."

The historic apple varieties making the grade are Newtown Pippins, Black Twig, Esopus Spitzenberg, Black Amish, Ashmead Kernel, and Calville Blanc, which is already producing in its fifth year of growth. Law says, "Calville makes a wonderful dessert apple. It has a sweet-sour, spicy lemon flavor and is moderately juicy." In the first year of production at Linden, Calville shows itself to be a very large, greenish yellow apple with a red blush. And its flavor, according to Law, is definitely worth savoring.

While Law is not going the organic route (he sprays his trees in spring to protect them against fungal diseases), he does not spray after the apples start to form in summer. In the fall, Linden's turns into a pick-your-own operation, and Law plans to keep it that way. "Growing modern hybrids is not a direction we want to go. Keeping the orchard small allows us to focus on the heirloom varieties. We look for the apples with the most personality and flavor. Our customers expect it." Note: Recipes from Jim Law are on pages 82 and 87.

Braised Duck with Vegetables

This is a superb company dish that can be prepared two or more days ahead of time. The advantage of cooking duck in advance is that all the fat can be removed from the juices when the duck is chilled. Because this dish is redolent with rich, earthy flavors, it is equally delicious when served with mashed potatoes and Brussels sprouts or rice with mushrooms and peas. With a mixed green salad on the side, the only dessert you'll need is a light and fruity sorbet.

DUCK AND STOCK

- 1 5½–6-pound duckling (plus neck, gizzard, heart, and liver)
- 4 cups stock or water
- 4 cloves of garlic, flattened
- 1 stalk of celery
- 1 small onion, halved
- 1 carrot, cut up

1. FOR THE STOCK, place the neck, gizzard, heart, and liver in a medium-sized saucepan and cover with the stock. Add 2 of the cloves of garlic, celery, onion, and carrot. Bring to a boil, reduce the heat, place the lid askew, and simmer for 40 minutes.

2. Cut the duck into serving-sized pieces, and remove any fat from around the neck and vent areas. Cut off the wing tips and parson's nose (stubby tailpiece) and discard.

3. In a 4- or 5-quart Dutch oven, brown the duck pieces, skin side down (do not use any fat or oil), over medium-high heat for 20 minutes to render the fat. Add the remaining 2 cloves of garlic to the pan during the browning.

4. Remove the duck pieces to a plate. Discard the garlic and the fat drippings.

VEGETABLES

- 2 tablespoons olive oil
- 1 large onion, chopped
- 2 medium carrots, chopped
- 2 medium stalks of celery, chopped
- 2 cloves of garlic, minced
- 1 teaspoon ground mace
- 1 teaspoon dried sage
- 1 teaspoon dried thyme
- ½ teaspoon ground allspice
- ¼ teaspoon freshly ground black pepper
- ⅛ teaspoon cayenne pepper
- 1 cup red wine
- 2 tablespoons cornstarch
- 3 apples (Granny Smith, Ida Red, Winesap, York)

5. FOR THE VEGETABLES, heat the olive oil in a Dutch oven over medium heat; add the onion, carrots, celery, and minced garlic. Sprinkle with the mace, sage, thyme, allspice, pepper, and cayenne. Sauté for 10 minutes.

6. Place the browned duck pieces, skin side up, on top of the vegetables in the Dutch oven.

7. Strain the stock and skim off the fat. (I use one of those fat jugs that allows fats to rise to the top. Or I make the stock a day ahead, refrigerate it, and then scrape the solid fat from the chilled liquid.)

8. Preheat oven to 325°F.

9. Add the wine to the stock and pour over the duck and vegetables. Cover the pot and roast for 1 hour to 1 hour 15 minutes. (At this point, the duck can be refrigerated for a day or two, so that any remaining fat can solidify and be scraped off.)

10. Place the Dutch oven on top of the stove and simmer for 15 minutes.

11. Remove the duck pieces to a dish, cover, and keep warm. Place the vegetables and liquid in a blender with the cornstarch. Purée until smooth and return to the Dutch oven with the duck pieces.

12. Peel, core, and cut the apples into ½-inch cubes. Stir the apples into the mixture in the Dutch oven; cover and bake for 20 to 30 minutes, or until the apples are tender.

Yield: 4 servings

Pork Chops with Apple Cream Sauce

This is an easy and good way to cook pork chops — the lean flesh gains moisture by absorbing the liquids. You can serve the sauce as it comes out of the skillet or you may decide to purée the apple slices to make a saucier cream sauce. This is a good dish to serve with rice.

1 tablespoon olive oil

4 center-cut loin pork chops, cut 1-inch thick and patted dry

3 large cloves of garlic, minced

freshly ground black pepper

1 tablespoon butter or olive oil

3 apples (Golden Delicious, Empire, Braeburn, Gala), cored, peeled and sliced ½–1-inch thick.

1 tablespoon brown sugar

1½ teaspoons ground mace

⅛ teaspoon ground cloves

⅛ teaspoon ground ginger

½ cup light cream or sour cream thinned with a drop of milk

¼ cup apple juice or cider

1. In a large skillet, heat the olive oil over medium heat. Add the pork chops and garlic, sprinkle with pepper to taste and brown for 2 minutes on each side. Remove to a plate.

2. Discard any fat in the skillet and heat the butter over medium heat. Add the apple slices; sprinkle with the sugar, mace, cloves, and ginger, and sauté for about 5 minutes, until softened and golden.

3. Add the cream and apple juice to the skillet, and when the mixture begins to bubble in about 3–5 minutes, add the pork chops. Reduce heat to low, cover the skillet and simmer for 15 minutes, until the chops are tender when pierced with a fork.

4. Remove the chops to a serving dish and cover with the sauce.

Yield: 4 servings

Pork Tenderloin Stuffed with Apples

This recipe is another favorite of Jim Law of Linden Vineyards. You can replace the butter with olive oil, but the flavor will not be quite as rich. The stuffing can also be used in split boneless chicken breasts, which you would bake for 20–25 minutes only.

1   pork tenderloin (about 1 pound)

2   tablespoons butter or olive oil

2   medium apples (Jonagold, Stayman, Winesap, Fuji), cored, peeled (if desired), and thinly sliced

1   medium onion, chopped

1   cup fresh bread crumbs, made by processing 2 large slices stale bread

½   teaspoon marjoram

½   teaspoon savory

½   teaspoon freshly ground black pepper

½   teaspoon salt

½   teaspoon–1 tablespoon vegetable or olive oil

GLAZE

4   tablespoons honey

2   tablespoons brown sugar

2   tablespoons cider vinegar

1   tablespoon brown mustard

1. Split the tenderloin almost in half. Place it between two sheets of wax paper; pound it to about ½-inch thick.

2. Melt the butter in a skillet over medium heat. Add the apples and onion and sauté until lightly brown and soft, about 5 minutes. Add the bread crumbs, marjoram, and savory and toss with the apple-onion mixture until moistened through. Remove from the heat.

3. Preheat oven to 375°F.

4. Pepper and salt the inside of the tenderloin and spread the apple stuffing over the surface.

5. Roll the tenderloin lengthwise and tie with kitchen string. Reheat the skillet over medium heat. Add the oil and brown the pork on all sides. Place in a baking dish.

6. To MAKE THE GLAZE, combine the honey, sugar, vinegar, and mustard.

7. Pour the glaze over the tenderloin and bake for 45 minutes, basting with the glaze 3–4 times. Remove from the oven; let stand for 5–10 minutes before serving.

Yield: 4 servings

Fragrant Lamb Stew

This is a good stew to serve with baked potatoes (regular bakers or sweet potatoes). Split the hot potatoes, fork up the flesh, and top with cooked broccoli florets tossed with sour cream and a little Dijon mustard.

2 tablespoons vegetable oil

2 medium carrots, diced

2 stalks of celery, diced

1 large onion, diced

3 cloves of garlic, minced

1 1-inch cube fresh ginger root, minced

½ teaspoon ground cinnamon

¼ teaspoon ground cloves

⅛ teaspoon cayenne pepper

4 pounds lean lamb shoulder, cut into 2-inch cubes

3 cups chicken or vegetable stock

1½ cups red wine or flat beer

2–3 tablespoons cornstarch

3 tablespoons cold water

2 large apples (Granny Smith, Braeburn, Fuji)

1. Heat the oil in a 6-quart Dutch oven and sauté the carrots, celery, onion, garlic, and ginger for 10 minutes. Sprinkle with the cinnamon, cloves, and cayenne.

2. Add the lamb and pour in the stock and wine. Cover the pot and simmer for 1½ hours.

3. Mix the cornstarch and water to a paste and stir into the stew to thicken to the desired consistency.

4. Peel, core, and cube the apples, add to the lamb, and simmer for 30 minutes longer.

Yield: 8–10 servings

Beef and Apple Deep-Dish Pie

My mother varied this traditional pork pie by using beef because the meat breaks down better during cooking, making for more tender bites.

¼ cup all-purpose flour

1 teaspoon dried thyme

½ teaspoon ground cinnamon

½ teaspoon ground ginger

½ teaspoon ground mace

½ teaspoon freshly ground
   black pepper

2 pounds boneless chuck or
   beef round, cut into
   1-inch chunks

5 tablespoons olive oil

2 large onions, thinly sliced

2 cups beef stock

1 cup red wine

2 medium apples (Granny
   Smith, Baldwin, Fuji)

pastry for a single piecrust
   (page 114)

1. Mix the flour with the thyme, cinnamon, ginger, mace, and pepper. Dredge the beef chunks in the spiced flour and reserve any flour that is left.

2. Heat 2 tablespoons of the oil in a Dutch oven and sauté half of the beef until browned on all sides. Remove to a plate. Brown the remaining beef in 2 tablespoons of oil.

3. Heat the remaining 1 tablespoon of oil in the Dutch oven and sauté the onions for 5 minutes. Add the remaining spiced flour to the onions and cook for 5 minutes.

4. Add the stock and wine; cook over medium heat until steaming. Scrape up any browned flour sticking to the sides.

5. Add the beef, cover the pot, and simmer over very low heat for 1 hour.

6. During the last 15 minutes, preheat oven to 400°F. Peel, core, and thinly slice the apples. Roll out the pastry to fit a deep 2-quart casserole dish.

7. Spoon the beef into the casserole dish, cover with the sliced apples, and top with the pastry. Seal the edges to the rim with the tines of a fork. Cut a small steam hole in the center.

8. Bake for 45 minutes, or until the crust is golden brown.

Yield: 6 servings

Louise Salinger's Apple Meat Loaf

I met Louise when I was living in Westchester County, New York. She used to provide great meals for her husband, Bob, and son, Bruce, who were running Salinger's Orchard in nearby Brewster. Today, Louise still lives in the middle of the orchard, which is now run by her son and his wife, Maureen, who is head baker for the orchard's market. According to Bruce, his mom's meat loaf is still one of his favorites. Louise, of course, makes her own applesauce.

3 small slices fresh bread, crumbled (about 1½ cups)

1 medium onion

1 pound ground beef

1 pound ground veal or pork

¼ cup ketchup

1 egg

2½ teaspoons prepared mustard

½ teaspoon pepper

1 cup applesauce

3 tablespoons apple cider

3 tablespoons brown sugar

1. Preheat oven to 350°F.

2. Crumble the bread into a large mixing bowl.

3. Grate in the onion. Add the beef, veal, ketchup, egg, 1½ teaspoons of the mustard, and pepper.

4. Mix well and shape into a round loaf. Place in a baking pan and bake for 1 hour.

5. In a small saucepan, heat the applesauce, cider, brown sugar, and the remaining 1 teaspoon mustard.

6. Pour over the meat loaf and for bake 30 minutes longer.

Yield: 4–6 servings

Curried Apple Meat Loaf

*This meat mixture makes delicious meatballs, too. Just shape
the meat into 2-inch balls and brown in 1 tablespoon oil
in a small Dutch oven. Drain off the fat, add ½ cup
tomato sauce, cover the pan, and bake for 30 minutes.*

2 slices whole-wheat bread

1 medium onion

1 large tart apple (Granny Smith, Jonagold, York)

1 pound ground beef

1 pound ground pork

½ cup raisins (optional)

½ cup plain yogurt

2 tablespoons steak sauce

1 egg

2 teaspoons curry powder

1 teaspoon dried thyme

GRAVY

1 teaspoon cornstarch

1 teaspoon curry powder

2 tablespoons apple juice

1. Preheat oven to 350°F.

2. Crumble the bread slices into a large mixing bowl. Grate in the onion.

3. Peel, core, and finely chop the apple. Add to the bowl.

4. Add the rest of the ingredients and mix well. (I use my hands and squish it together.) Turn into a 9- by 5-inch loaf pan, cover, and bake for 1 hour.

5. TO MAKE THE GRAVY, pour the pan juices into a skillet. Mix the cornstarch, curry powder, and apple juice until smooth. Add to the pan juices, heat, and stir until thickened. To make thicker gravy, use 2 teaspoons cornstarch; for thinner gravy, add a little milk.

Yield: 6 servings

Polish Sausage, Apples, and Red Cabbage

The vegetables are in the pot, so all you'll need is to serve this with steamed or microwaved potatoes and crusty French bread.

2 tablespoons olive oil

2 medium onions, thinly sliced

2 cloves of garlic, minced

1 medium red cabbage, shredded

4 apples (Granny Smith, Fuji, Jonagold, Braeburn)

2½ pounds kielbasa (Polish sausage) or low-fat turkey kielbasa

1 bay leaf

1 teaspoon dried thyme

½ teaspoon ground mace

½ teaspoon freshly ground black pepper

½ cup beef, chicken, or vegetable stock

1 tablespoon red wine or apple cider vinegar

1. Heat the oil in a 4-quart kettle and sauté the onions and garlic for 5 minutes.

2. Stir the cabbage into the onions and sauté for 5 minutes.

3. Peel, core, and slice the apples, and add to the pot. Stir all together.

4. Put the kielbasa into the pot with the vegetables. Add the bay leaf and sprinkle with the thyme, mace, and pepper.

5. Add the stock and vinegar, cover the pot, and bring to a boil. Reduce the heat and simmer for 30–40 minutes.

6. Meanwhile, warm a serving platter. Remove the kielbasa and cut into serving-sized portions. Arrange the vegetables on the serving platter; top with the kielbasa.

Yield: 4–6 servings

Curried Ham and Apples

I have found this to be a crowd-pleaser, which means I have tripled the recipe. It's an easy dish to make when you have guests and return home after a day out. Have your guests peel and dice the apples; it's a nice way for them to contribute to the meal without getting in the way of your preparations. Serve with jasmine rice, a mixed salad, crusty bread, and a fruity red wine such as an Australian shiraz or a California pinot noir. Cheers!

2 tablespoons olive oil or butter

2 tablespoons flour

1 tablespoon mild curry powder

2¼ cups milk

2 medium sweet apples (Golden Delicious, Mutsu/Crispin, Empire, Gala)

½ cup raisins

one 1-pound, center-cut slice fully cooked ham, cut ¾-inch thick

1. Heat the oil in a medium-sized skillet. Stir in the flour and curry powder and cook for 1 minute.

2. Pour in the milk and, using a wooden spoon or wire whisk, stir to make a smooth sauce.

3. Peel, core, and dice the apples. Add to the curry sauce with the raisins. Cook over low heat for 10 minutes.

4. Cube the ham (remove fat and bone, if necessary) and stir into the pan. Cook for 10 minutes longer, or until heated through.

Yield: 2–3 servings

APPLE FIGURES

For those of you who enjoy statistics, here's how apples stack up:

- The six top apple-producing states in the United States are Washington, New York, Michigan, California, Pennsylvania, and Virginia.
- The 2000 U.S. apple crop was estimated to be 254.217 million 42-pound cartons.
- The largest U.S. apple crop on record is 277.3 million cartons, harvested in 1998.
- In 1997, there were 9,000 U.S. apple growers and 453,200 acres of commercial orchards.
- Apples trailed only oranges and grapes in the amount of U.S. acreage committed to fruit production in 1997.
- In 1999, the average U.S. consumer ate an estimated 18.7 pounds of fresh apples and 29.7 pounds of processed apples.
- In 1999, the People's Republic of China produced the world's largest crop of apples. The United States was the world's second-largest producer, with Turkey, Italy, and France completing the list of the world's top five apple-producing countries.
- The United States, New Zealand, and Japan are the leaders in apple breeding.

APPLE TIPS

When cooking with apples, it's handy to know that:

- 1 pound of apples yields 4 cups when chopped or sliced, and 1½ cups of applesauce.
- 1 pound of apples may contain 4 small, 3 medium, or 2 large apples.
- Apple juice and apple cider can be used interchangeably in recipes.
- 2–2½ pounds of apples will suffice for a 9- or 10-inch pie. That means 9–10 small apples, 7–8 medium apples, or 5 large ones.
- Overripe apples, once the bruises have been removed, make good applesauce or cider.
- Underripe apples can be chopped, diced, sliced, and grated for sautéing with vegetables or for putting into cakes, muffins, pies, and other cooked dishes.
- Sliced or cut apples will stay white longer if dropped into a bowl of water containing 2 tablespoons of lemon juice. (Cortland and Golden Delicious do not discolor as quickly as other varieties.)
- When recipes call for unpeeled apples, the apples always should be washed first. That not only ensures the removal of dirt or contaminants accumulated during handling and transportation, but eliminates the possibility of residual pesticide consumption.

NOTHING SEEMS TO MEET WITH MORE APPRECIATION than a fresh-baked apple pie. Fresh apples, fragrant with cinnamon and lightly sugared, fill a tender, flaky pastry. Although "easy as pie" doesn't seem as easy today as it did to our grandmothers, pies are so yummy and beautiful that it is worth the effort to master the making. If you are more comfortable with batter, there are lots of scrumptious apple cakes that will fill your kitchen with good baking smells.

APPLE
Pies & Cakes

Harvest Apple Pie

This is my basic apple pie; the only way I vary it is by using different apples (sometimes I use more than one variety) or by rolling out a very large circle of pastry, placing it in a pizza pan, and folding the pastry over the apples to create a very large, half-moon shaped pie.

pastry for a double 9- or 10-inch piecrust (pages 113–115)

¼ cup melted apricot jam or marmalade

5 large apples (Ida Red, Jonathan, Golden Delicious, or a mix of several varieties)

2 tablespoons lemon juice

½ cup firmly packed brown sugar

2 tablespoons all-purpose flour

½ teaspoon cinnamon

¼ teaspoon nutmeg

1 tablespoon butter

1½ teaspoons milk

1 teaspoon granulated sugar

1. Preheat oven to 400°F and grease a 9- or 10-inch pie plate.

2. Roll out half of the pastry and fit it into the pie plate. Brush with the melted jam and refrigerate.

3. Peel, core, and cut the apples into ¼-inch slices. Place in a bowl and toss with the lemon juice.

4. Combine the brown sugar, flour, cinnamon, and nutmeg.

5. Layer half of the apple slices in the chilled pie shell and sprinkle with half of the sugar mixture. Repeat the layers. Cut the butter into small pieces and scatter over the apples.

6. Roll out the top crust, place over the filling, trim and flute the edges. Cut 3 steam vents in the center.

7. Brush with the milk and sprinkle with the granulated sugar.

8. Bake in the middle of the oven for 50–60 minutes. If the edges of the crust start to brown too quickly, cover with strips of aluminum foil. Let cool for at least 10 minutes before serving.

Yield: 8 servings

French Apple Tart

A lovely, citrus-accented apple tart that I always vow I'll make more often, because it is so delicious and also so easy to assemble.

pastry for a single 10-inch piecrust (page 113)

1 egg white, beaten

10 large apples (Mutsu/Crispin, Winesap, Jonagold, or a mix of 14–15 Golden Delicious and Braeburn)

2 tablespoons lemon juice

2 tablespoons granulated sugar

½ cup brown sugar

¼ cup orange, lemon, or apple marmalade

2 tablespoons brandy (optional)

2 tablespoons butter

¼ cup apple jelly or marmalade

1. Preheat oven to 400°F. Grease a 10-inch pie plate or flan tin.

2. Roll out the pastry and fit it into the pie plate. Flute the edges, brush the bottom with the egg white, and then refrigerate.

3. Peel, core, and cut the apples into ½-inch slices. Place half the apples in a 3- or 4-quart saucepan (don't overcrowd the apples, or it will take longer for the juice to evaporate). Place the remainder in a medium-sized bowl. Add the lemon juice and granulated sugar to the bowl; toss to coat the apples.

4. To the apple slices in the saucepan, add the brown sugar, orange marmalade, brandy, if desired, and butter. Cover the pan and cook over low heat for 15 minutes. Remove the cover, beat the mixture, and cook for 5–10 minutes longer. The mixture should be thick and smooth. Remove from the heat and cool.

5. When the applesauce has cooled slightly, spoon it into the chilled pie shell and arrange the tossed apple slices decoratively on top. Bake for 15 minutes. Reduce the heat to 350°F and bake for 30 minutes longer.

6. Melt the apple jelly and brush over the baked apple slices. Allow to cool slightly before serving.

Yield: 8 servings

Apple Nut Puff Tarts

*I often turn to this recipe when I want to serve "apple pie"
to family and friends but find I'm short on time. I use a sheet of
frozen puff pastry or the little frozen shells. Call these tarts fast food,
if you will, but they are delicious. I vary the flavor by using black
walnuts or pecans and adding grated citrus zest. Serve with
vanilla ice cream or frozen yogurt.*

1 sheet frozen puff pastry

1 can (21 ounces) apple-pie
filling

½ cup chopped black walnuts,
regular walnuts, or
pecans, toasted

1 teaspoon grated orange,
lime, or lemon zest

¼ cup raisins, plumped in
apple juice or brandy
(optional)

2 tablespoons marmalade, or
apricot preserves

1. Preheat oven to 375°F.

2. Place the pastry on a lightly floured surface and roll into a 12-inch square. Using a sharp knife or pastry or pizza cutter, slice the pastry into four 6-inch squares, and set them on a baking sheet.

3. Pinch ½ inch around the edges of each square, bringing the pastry up to form a lip. Prick the crust in several places with the tines of a fork. Place in the freezer for a few minutes to firm up if the pastry seems too soft.

4. Bake the tart cases for 10–15 minutes, until they are golden and crisp. Keep an eye on them, and if they seem to be puffing up too much, press the pastry down with the back of a spoon. Remove from the oven and transfer to a serving plate.

5. While the pastry is baking, combine the apple-pie filling with the nuts and orange zest; add the raisins, if desired.

6. Melt the marmalade in a small saucepan over low heat.

7. Spread a spoonful of the marmalade over the pastry, and spoon the pie filling into the tart cases.

Yield: 4 servings

VARIATIONS

For little tarts, use a package of frozen puff pastry shells, thawed and baked according to package directions. Brush with marmalade and fill as directed.

If you want to make your own filling, peel, core, and slice 4 apples and sauté in 2 teaspoons of butter over medium heat in a covered skillet for 10 minutes, until soft.

APPLE PICKING TIPS

If you are interested in getting the freshest apples you can buy, then picking your own (page 36) is the way to go. Here are some tips to get you started:

- Call the orchard ahead to check which varieties will be ready for harvesting and whether there are picnic areas and other facilities.

- Take your own bags and baskets unless the orchard specifically states that they provide containers.

- Pick apples by giving them a half twist back and forth. This loosens the stem gently without damaging the branch.

- When harvesting fallen apples, check for bruises, ants, and wasps.

- Wear long-sleeved shirts and long pants to avoid getting stung by wasps and bees that may be feasting on apples pecked open by birds.

- Wear comfortable boots or high-top sneakers.

- Apply sunblock. Sunny days in fall can be deceptively hot.

- Before munching on a just-picked apple, ask the orchardist whether fungal or other sprays have been used recently. If so, wash it before eating.

Apple Cream Cheese Tart

This scrumptious apple cheesecake in a tart shell is a recipe I received from Ann Kojis Ziff, my longtime friend, who used to bake me the most wonderful birthday cakes when I first came to the United States.

½ cup (1 stick) butter

¾ cup granulated sugar

1 teaspoon lemon juice

1 cup sifted all-purpose flour

1 pound cream cheese

½ cup brown sugar

1 egg

2 teaspoons vanilla extract

2 large apples (Cortland, Rome Beauty, Jonathan, Fuji)

1 teaspoon ground cinnamon

1. In a large bowl, cream together the butter, ¼ cup of the granulated sugar, and lemon juice. Stir in the flour until well blended.

2. Press the dough into the bottom and about 1½ inches up the sides of a 9-inch springform pan. Refrigerate.

3. Preheat oven to 425°F.

4. Place cream cheese and brown sugar in a mixing bowl; beat until fluffy. Add egg and vanilla. Beat until smooth.

5. Peel, core, and cut the apples into ¼-inch slices.

6. In a large bowl, combine the remaining ½ cup granulated sugar and the cinnamon. Add the apple slices and toss until coated.

7. Pour the cream cheese filling into the prepared shell and cover with the sugared apple slices.

8. Bake for 15 minutes, reduce oven to 350°F, and bake for 40–45 minutes longer.

9. Remove from the oven and cool on a wire rack. Use a knife to loosen the tart before removing the pan sides.

Yield: 10–12 servings

Pumpkin Apple Pie

If you have a hard time choosing between pumpkin pie
and apple pie, you'll want to try this one. It makes a wonderful
combination for an autumn dinner. You can easily substitute
canned apple slices for the sautéed fresh apples.

pastry for a single 10-inch
   piecrust (page 113)

2 medium apples (Granny
      Smith, Braeburn,
      Newtown Pippin,
      Northern Spy) or 2 cups
      drained canned apple
      slices

1 teaspoon butter

2 cups pumpkin purée,
      canned or fresh

1½ cups light cream or
      half-and-half

1 cup brown sugar

2 eggs

1 teaspoon ground cinnamon

½ teaspoon ground nutmeg

¼ teaspoon ground cloves

¼ teaspoon ground ginger

1. Preheat oven to 425°F. Grease a 10-inch pie plate.

2. Roll out the pastry and fit it into the pie plate. Trim and flute the edges. Refrigerate.

3. Peel, core, and cut the apples into ¼-inch slices. Place in a skillet with the butter, cover, and cook over low heat for 5 minutes. Remove from the heat and drain. If you are using canned apples, simply drain and set aside.

4. Place the pumpkin, cream, sugar, eggs, cinnamon, nutmeg, cloves, and ginger in a medium-sized mixing bowl. Beat together until smooth.

5. Arrange the apple slices in the bottom of the chilled pastry shell and pour the pumpkin mixture over them.

6. Bake for 15 minutes. Reduce oven to 375°F and bake for 35–40 minutes longer, or until a knife inserted into the center comes out clean. Allow to cool before serving.

Yield: 8–10 servings

Apple Raspberry Pie

Apples and raspberries go well together, perhaps better than any other apple combination. At least I think that until I taste apples and peaches, apples and strawberries, or apples and cranberries.

pastry for a double piecrust
(pages 113–115)

1 tablespoon raspberry jam

1 package (12 ounces) frozen
raspberries, thawed and
drained with the juice
reserved

1½ tablespoons cornstarch

¼ cup plus ⅓ cup sugar

¼ cup all-purpose flour

4 large apples (Rome Beauty)

Note: If you use fresh raspberries, you will need 1½–2 cups of berries plus ½ cup apple or apple-raspberry juice to use in step 3.

1. Preheat oven to 425°F. Grease a 9- or 10-inch pie plate.

2. Roll out half of the pastry and fit it into the pie plate. Smooth the raspberry jam over the bottom of the pie shell. Refrigerate.

3. Pour the reserved juice from the raspberries into a small saucepan; stir in the cornstarch and ¼ cup of the sugar.

4. Bring the cornstarch mixture to a boil over low heat, stirring until the juice is thick and smooth. Remove from the heat, stir in the drained raspberries, and cool.

5. Combine the flour and the remaining ⅓ cup sugar.

6. Peel, core, and cut the apples into ¼-inch slices.

7. Alternate layers of apple slices and the flour mixture in the chilled pie shell. Top with the cooled raspberry mixture.

8. Roll out the top crust, place over the filling, trim and flute the edges. Cut 3 vents in the center.

9. Bake for 15 minutes, reduce oven to 350°F, and bake for 30–40 minutes longer, until the crust is golden brown. If the edges start to brown too quickly, cover with strips of aluminum foil. Allow the pie to set for at least 30 minutes before serving. Serve warm, with English Custard Sauce (page 152) or vanilla ice cream.

Yield: 8 servings

Apple Cranberry Meringue Pie

Another recipe given to me by my good friend Ann Kojis Ziff when we worked together in New York City. With its pretty pink interior and lightly golden swirled meringue crust, it is a festive holiday pie.

pastry for a single 9-inch piecrust (page 114)

1 egg white, at room temperature, beaten

3 medium apples (Ida Red, Empire, Golden Delicious)

½ cup brown sugar

¼ cup all-purpose flour

½ teaspoon ground cinnamon

½ teaspoon ground ginger

2 cups fresh cranberries

½ cup granulated sugar

MERINGUE TOPPING

3 egg whites, at room temperature

¼ teaspoon cream of tartar

½ cup granulated sugar

1. Preheat oven to 425°F. Grease a 9-inch pie plate.

2. Roll out the pastry; fit it into the pie plate. Flute the edges. Brush the egg white over the pastry. Refrigerate.

3. Peel, core, and cut the apples into ¼-inch slices. Place in a medium-sized bowl. Mix the brown sugar, flour, cinnamon, and ginger. Toss with the apple slices and put into the crust.

4. Combine the cranberries and granulated sugar. Using a fork, lightly crush the cranberries. Spread over the apples.

5. Cover the filling with a piece of aluminum foil in which a ½-inch hole has been cut in the middle. Bake for 15 minutes. Reduce oven to 350°F and bake 45 minutes longer.

6. TO MAKE THE MERINGUE TOPPING, place the 3 egg whites and cream of tartar in a medium-sized bowl. Using an electric mixer, beat until foamy. Gradually add the remaining ½ cup sugar — 2 tablespoons at a time — beating continuously. When the whites are stiff, spread over the hot filling, bringing the meringue to the edges of the crust to form a seal. Return the pie to the oven and bake for 12–15 minutes longer at 350°F, until golden. Allow the pie to set for at least 30 minutes before serving.

Yield: 8 servings

Mother's Apple and Brambleberry Deep-Dish Pie

Brambleberry is the British name for blackberries, which make a dark, juicy filling. When she thinks she needs to make a variation on pie, my mother will make this into a cobbler, which is actually easier, because the dough doesn't require rolling.

5   large apples (Rhode Island Greening, Granny Smith, Fuji)

1   cup sugar

½   cups blackberries or brambleberries

pastry for a single piecrust (pages 113–114)

1   egg white, beaten

Note: This pie is very juicy, because no thickener is added. If you prefer a thicker consistency, mix 3 tablespoons flour with the sugar.

1. Preheat oven to 400°F. Grease a 2-quart casserole dish or soufflé dish.

2. Peel, core, and cut the apples into ¼-inch slices. Layer half in the dish.

3. Sprinkle with ½ cup of the sugar. Cover with the berries, then the remaining sugar. Finish with the apple slices.

4. Roll out the pastry 1½ inches larger than the dish. Cover the filling with the pastry, turn under the overhang, trimming where necessary, and press firmly to the rim of the dish. Make a pattern around the edges, if desired, with the tines of a fork.

5. Cut 3 steam vents in the crust and brush with the egg white to glaze. Bake for 40 minutes or until the pastry is golden. If the edges start to brown too quickly, cover with strips of aluminum foil. Allow the pie to cool and serve with English Custard Sauce (page 152).

Yield: 8 servings

Apple Crumb Pie

This recipe was given to me by Louise Salinger of Salinger's Orchard in Brewster, New York. Having been married to an orchardist for 40 years and having raised a family, Louise knows more about apples and pies than anyone else I've met. Her daughter-in-law, Maureen, who is head baker for Salinger's Orchard Apple Market, comes in a very close second.

pastry for a single 10-inch piecrust (page 113)

5 large apples (Northern Spy, Rhode Island Greening, Fuji)

1½ cups sour cream

¾ cup granulated sugar

¾ cup all-purpose flour

1 large egg

2 teaspoons vanilla extract

½ cup brown sugar

½ cup (1 stick) butter

1 cup chopped pecans

1. Preheat oven to 450°F. Grease a 10-inch pie plate.

2. Roll out the pastry and fit it into the pie plate. Flute the edges and refrigerate.

3. Peel, core, and cut the apples into ¼-inch slices. Arrange in the chilled pie shell.

4. In a small bowl, combine the sour cream, granulated sugar, ¼ cup of the flour, egg, and vanilla. Beat until smooth and pour over the apple slices.

5. Bake for 10 minutes, reduce oven to 350°F, and bake for 30 minutes longer.

6. Mix the remaining ½ cup flour, brown sugar, and butter until the mixture is crumbly. Stir in the pecans and sprinkle over the baked pie.

7. Return the pie to the oven and bake 15 minutes longer, or until the topping is golden brown.

Yield: 8 servings

Apple, Rhubarb, and Strawberry Streusel Pie

With streusel oat crumb topping and base sandwiching a luscious combination of fruits, this is a most satisfying crumble pie.

2 cups old-fashioned rolled oats

½ cup brown sugar

½ cup (1 stick) butter, melted

¾ cup granulated sugar

⅓ cup all-purpose flour

½ teaspoon ground ginger

¼ teaspoon ground nutmeg

2 medium apples (Golden Delicious, Empire)

2 cups sliced rhubarb

2 cups whole strawberries, hulled

1. Preheat oven to 425°F. Grease a 10-inch pie plate.

2. In a medium-sized bowl, combine the oats, brown sugar, and butter. Blend well.

3. Take two-thirds of the mixture and press firmly into the bottom and up the sides of the pie plate. Refrigerate.

4. Mix the granulated sugar, flour, ginger, and nutmeg in a large bowl.

5. Peel, core, and cut the apples into ¼-inch slices.

6. Toss the apples, rhubarb, and strawberries with the sugar and flour mixture and pour into the chilled streusel base. Sprinkle with the remaining streusel crumbs.

7. Bake for 15 minutes. Reduce oven to 375°F and bake for 30 minutes longer or until golden brown. Let cool before serving.

Yield: 8 servings

Hank Keenan's Peach and Apple Deep-Dish Pie

Hank is a photographer who also sells apples at Salinger's Orchard in Brewster, New York. When I was buying apples and peaches toward the end of a particularly beautiful summer, Hank described the apple and peach pie he'd made that weekend. It sounded so delicious that when I arrived home I reconstructed it — he hadn't worked from a recipe.

5 medium apples (Cortland, Golden Delicious, Honeycrisp, Braeburn)

¾ cup sugar

¼ cup instant tapioca

2 teaspoons grated lemon zest

½ teaspoon ground cinnamon

½ teaspoon ground ginger

½ teaspoon ground nutmeg

5 medium peaches

pastry for a single piecrust (pages 113–116

1. Preheat oven to 400°F. Grease a 2-quart casserole dish.

2. Peel, core, and cut the apples into ¼-inch slices. Put into a bowl.

3. Mix the sugar, tapioca, lemon zest, cinnamon, ginger, and nutmeg. Sprinkle the apple slices with the spice mixture and toss until completely coated.

4. Remove the pits from the peaches and cut into ½-inch slices. Place in a separate bowl.

5. Starting with the apple slices, layer the apples and peaches in the greased dish.

6. Roll out the pastry 1½ inches larger than the casserole dish. Cover the filling with the pastry, turn under the overhang, trim where necessary, and press firmly to the rim of the dish. Make a pattern around the edges, if desired, with the tines of a fork.

7. Cut 3 steam vents in the crust and bake for 40 minutes, or until the pastry is golden. If the edges start to brown too quickly, cover with strips of aluminum foil. Let the pie cool before serving.

Yield: 8–10 servings

Cheese and Apple Tartlets

The homemade apple purée is like a thick, smooth sauce.
You could also start with store-bought applesauce and cook it down
to a thicker consistency. Or you could use thick apple butter.

pastry for a single piecrust
(pages 113–116)

4 large apples (Granny
Smith, Empire, Golden
Delicious)

2–4 tablespoons sugar

½ teaspoon ground nutmeg

¾ cup grated Cheddar
cheese

1. Preheat oven to 350°F. Grease 12 small muffin cups or a tin tartlet pan.

2. Roll out the pastry to a rectangle ⅛-inch thick. Using a 3-inch round pastry cutter, cut out 12 circles and fit into the muffin cups. Pat the pastry up the sides and around the rims of the cups and press down with the tines of a fork.

3. Prick the base of each crust with a fork and fill each with crumpled aluminum foil or dried beans. Bake for 15 minutes. Remove the foil or beans and bake for 5 minutes longer. Remove and cool on a wire rack.

4. Peel, core, and slice the apples. Put into a saucepan, cover, and cook slowly until soft, approximately 20 minutes. Remove the lid and cook 5–10 minutes longer, until the moisture has evaporated.

5. Add the sugar and nutmeg. Stir until the mixture is like a thick purée. Cool.

6. Preheat the broiler. Fill the cool tartlet crusts with the cool apple purée. Top with the Cheddar and broil for 1 minute to melt the cheese. Serve warm or cooled.

Yield: 12 small tartlets

Apple Envelope

*I love the rustic look of this pie, and I like how fast it is to make.
And it's faster still if I opt to use frozen puff or phyllo pastry. The
flavorings are very basic; if you like, you can add ½ teaspoon each
of ground nutmeg and ginger. Or replace the allspice with
1 teaspoon cinnamon. Or add grated orange or lemon zest.*

3 medium apples (McIntosh,
   Golden Delicious, Empire,
   Gala)

¼ cup raisins

2 tablespoons honey

1 teaspoon ground allspice

   pastry for a single 9-inch
    piecrust (pages 114–116)

   milk

   sugar

1. Preheat oven to 400°F. Grease a large baking sheet.

2. Peel, core, and cut the apples into ¼-inch slices.

3. In a medium-sized bowl, combine the apples with the raisins, honey, and allspice.

4. Roll out the pastry to a circle approximately 10 inches in diameter.

5. Spoon the apple mixture over half the dough, leaving a 1-inch border. Fold the other half over the apples, moisten the edges with milk, and seal. Crimp the edges with the tines or the handle of a fork.

6. Place on the baking sheet, brush with milk, and sprinkle with sugar.

7. Bake for 45 minutes. Serve warm with English Custard Sauce (page 152) or heavy cream.

Yield: 2 servings

Apple Pizza

*This is really a single-crust tart, but using mozzarella as a cheese base
makes it more like a pizza — a special sweet pizza.*

pastry for a single piecrust
  (pages 113–116)

5 large apples (Winesap,
  Rome Beauty, Fuji,
  Jonagold)

½ cup grated Cheddar,
  mozzarella, or Swiss
  cheese

½ cup brown sugar

½ cup chopped walnuts

½ teaspoon ground cinnamon

½ teaspoon ground nutmeg

2 tablespoons butter

1. Preheat oven to 400°F. Grease a 12-inch pizza pan.

2. Roll the pastry into a 13-inch circle and place in the greased pizza pan. Form a rim around the edges.

3. Bake for 10 minutes.

4. Peel, core, and cut the apples into ¼-inch slices. Arrange on the pizza crust and sprinkle with the Cheddar.

5. Mix the sugar, walnuts, cinnamon, and nutmeg. Sprinkle on top of the cheese.

6. Cut the butter into small pieces and dot over the top.

7. Bake for 20 minutes, or until the apples are tender. Serve hot.

Yield: 8 servings

APPLE LIQUIDS FOR BAKING

Apple juice adds a natural sweetness and moistness and can help you reduce fat in your baking. Your cakes will still be moist but much lower in fat. When beginning to experiment with eliminating some or most of the oil in baked goods, start by substituting apple sauce (other fruit purees work the same way) for one-quarter the amount of fat and then work up to one-half the fat called for in a recipe. I substitute applesauce 100 percent for the fat when making my healthiest breakfast breads and muffins. I prefer the enhanced flavor and the seemingly more moist texture.

Apple Turnovers

The simplest way to make turnovers is to use frozen puff pastry or a package of pastry crusts. However, homemade pastry is easy to make and is superior to most commercial pastry dough.

4 medium apples (McIntosh, Golden Delicious, Gala, Ginger Gold)
1 tablespoon lemon juice
2 tablespoons butter
⅓ cup sugar
1 tablespoon cornstarch
pastry for a double piecrust (pages 113–115)
milk

1. Grease a large baking sheet.

2. Peel, core, and cut the apples into ¼-inch slices. Place in a medium-sized bowl. Sprinkle with the lemon juice.

3. Cut the butter into small pieces; add to the apple slices.

4. Mix the sugar and cornstarch. Stir into the apple mixture.

5. Divide the pastry into 8 equal parts and roll into 6- or 7-inch squares.

6. Spoon the filling onto the center of each square. Brush the edges with milk and fold over to make a triangle.

7. Press the edges together to seal and crimp with the tines of a fork. Using a sharp knife, make a steam vent in the middle of each. Place on the baking sheet and refrigerate for 15 minutes.

8. Meanwhile, preheat oven to 425°F.

9. Brush the turnovers with milk and bake for 30 minutes, or until golden brown. Remove from the baking sheet and serve warm or cold.

Yield: 8 turnovers

Louise Salinger's Apple Pastry Squares

*Louise Salinger of Salinger's Orchard is a superb cook who loves
to bake. You'll find more of her recipes elsewhere in this book.*

2¾ cups sifted all-purpose flour

¾ cup (1½ sticks) butter

¼ cup milk

1 egg

8 medium apples (Granny Smith, Golden Delicious, Honeycrisp, Braeburn)

½ cup granulated sugar

1 teaspoon ground cinnamon

1 cup cereal flakes, e.g., cornflakes

milk, for brushing the pastry

1 cup confectioners' sugar

2 tablespoons water

1 teaspoon vanilla extract

1. In a medium-sized bowl, cut the butter into the flour with two knives or a pastry blender, or in a food processor.

2. Beat the milk and egg, then mix with the flour mixture to form a firm dough. Divide into 2 pieces and refrigerate.

3. Preheat oven to 400°F. Grease and flour a 15½-inch jelly-roll pan.

4. Peel, core, and thinly slice the apples into a medium-sized bowl. Mix with the granulated sugar and the cinnamon.

5. Roll out half of the dough to fit the bottom of the pan and sprinkle with the cereal flakes to within ½ inch of the edges.

6. Spoon the apple mixture on top of the flakes.

7. Roll out the remaining dough and place over the apples. Seal the edges by pinching together. Brush the pastry with a little milk.

8. Bake for 1 hour. Remove to a wire rack to cool.

9. While the pastry is still slightly warm, combine the confectioners' sugar, water, and vanilla. Spread over the pastry. Serve warm or cold.

Yield: 20 servings

Flaky Pastry

Although not as richly flavored as a crust made with all butter,
pastry made with vegetable shortening is more tender. This is one of
the most basic pastry doughs to make for piecrusts.

3 cups sifted all-purpose
    flour

1 cup vegetable shortening

3 tablespoons sugar
    (optional for sweet
    pastry)

½ cup ice water

    beaten egg white or jam
      or jelly*

    beaten egg or milk

    sugar (optional)

*Note: If the jam is too
solid or too cold to spread,
melt it first, but cool before
brushing onto the pastry.

1. Sift the flour into a medium-sized bowl. Cut in the shortening with 2 knives or a pastry blender, or in a food processor, until the mixture resembles coarse crumbs. (Add sugar, if desired.)

2. Using a fork, stir in the water, a tablespoon at a time, until the dough forms a ball. Too much water or overmixing will make the crust tough.

3. Divide the dough into 2 pieces and flatten into 6-inch circles. Wrap in wax paper and refrigerate for 30 minutes.

4. Roll out the pastry to a 12-inch circle about ⅛-inch thick. Loosely fold the circle in half, fit into a buttered pie plate (butter browns and crisps the pastry more than shortening), and trim, leaving a 1-inch overhang.

5. Brush the crust with beaten egg white to help prevent the bottom from becoming soggy. Refrigerate until the filling is ready.

6. Roll out the second piece of dough. Carefully lift the pastry and place over the filling. Trim, if necessary. Seal to the bottom crust. Flute the edges, cut two or three steam vents in the center, and brush with the beaten egg. Sprinkle with sugar, if desired. Bake according to the recipe directions.

Yield: Two 10-inch piecrusts, 8 dumplings, or
twelve 6-inch turnovers

Short Pastry

A really good basic pastry for piecrusts, this is called short pastry because of its high ratio of shortening to flour. If you substitute stick margarine for the shortening, work fast and handle the pastry only when necessary because margarine softens quickly.

2½ cups sifted all-purpose flour

6 tablespoons vegetable shortening

6 tablespoons butter

2 tablespoons sugar (optional for sweet pastry)

6 tablespoons ice water

beaten egg white or jam or jelly*

beaten egg or milk

sugar (optional)

*Note: If the jam is too solid or cold to spread, melt it first, but cool before brushing onto the pastry.

1. Sift the flour into a medium-sized bowl. Cut in the shortening and butter with two knives or a pastry blender, or in a food processor, until the mixture resembles coarse crumbs. (Add the sugar, if desired.)

2. Using a fork, stir in the water, a tablespoon at a time, until the dough forms a ball. Too much water or overmixing will make the crust tough.

3. Divide the dough into 2 pieces and flatten into 6-inch circles. Wrap in wax paper and refrigerate for 30 minutes.

4. Roll out the pastry to a 12-inch circle about ⅛-inch thick. Loosely fold the circle in half, fit into a buttered pie plate, and trim, leaving a 1-inch overhang.

5. Brush the crust with a beaten egg white to help prevent the bottom from becoming soggy. Refrigerate until the filling is ready.

6. Roll out the second piece of dough. Carefully lift the pastry and place over the filling. Trim, if necessary. Seal to the bottom crust. Flute the edges, cut two or three steam vents in the center, and brush with beaten egg. Sprinkle with sugar, if desired. Bake according to the recipe directions.

Yield: Two 9-inch piecrusts, 6 dumplings, or eight to ten 6-inch turnovers

Cheese Pastry

*Use this pastry for a change when making a plain
apple pie, apple turnovers, or dumplings.*

2½ cups sifted all-purpose
      flour

¾ cup vegetable shortening

½ cup grated Cheddar cheese

⅓–½ cup ice water

    beaten egg white or jam or
      jelly*

    beaten egg or milk

    sugar (optional)

*Note: If the jam is too
solid or too cold to spread,
melt it first, but cool
before brushing onto the
pastry.

1. Sift the flour into a medium-sized bowl and cut in the shortening with two knives or a pastry blender until coarse crumbs form. Stir in the Cheddar with a fork.

2. Using a fork, stir in the water, a tablespoon at a time, until the dough forms a ball. Too much water or overmixing will make the crust tough.

3. Divide the dough into 2 pieces and flatten into 6-inch circles. Wrap in wax paper and refrigerate for 30 minutes.

4. Roll out the pastry to a 12-inch circle about ⅛-inch thick. Loosely fold the circle in half, fit into a buttered pie plate, and trim, leaving a 1-inch overhang.

5. Brush the crust with a beaten egg white to help prevent the bottom from becoming soggy. Refrigerate until the filling is ready.

6. Roll out the second piece of dough. Carefully lift the pastry and place over the filling. Trim, if necessary. Seal to the bottom crust. Flute the edges, cut two or three steam vents in the center, and brush with beaten egg. Sprinkle with sugar, if desired. Bake according to the recipe directions.

**Yield: Two 9-inch piecrusts, 6 dumplings, or
eight to ten 6-inch turnovers**

Butter Piecrust

This is deliciously like shortbread cookies — rich and buttery.

1½ cups sifted all-purpose flour
½ cup (1 stick) butter
1 tablespoon sugar (optional)
¼ cup ice water
1 teaspoon lemon juice

1. Sift the flour into a medium-sized bowl and cut in the butter with two knives or a pastry blender, or in a food processor. (Add the sugar, if desired.)

2. Using a fork, stir in the water and lemon juice, 1 tablespoon at a time. When a ball forms, stop adding water, flatten, wrap in wax paper, and refrigerate for 30 minutes.

3. Roll out the pastry on a floured surface to a 12-inch circle, fold in half, and fit into the pie plate.

4. Trim so that a 1-inch overhang remains, turn under, pinch, and flute. Refrigerate until ready to use.

5. To bake an unfilled pie shell, prick the bottom and sides of the pastry with a fork to allow air to escape during baking. Bake in a preheated 450°F oven for 10 minutes (prebaked) or 20 minutes (fully baked).

Yield: 1 crust or 12 small tart shells

VARIATION: WHOLE-WHEAT CRUST

Substitute ⅓ cup whole-wheat flour for ½ cup all-purpose flour, and add a *drop* more water, if necessary.

Terri's Quick Apple Cake

Terri Booth, executive secretary for the U.S. Apple Association, calls this her "company's coming" cake. It's definitely a fast and winning recipe for a party or when you're expecting weekend guests. Terri's house is like an apple museum, featuring apple memorabilia in the thousands.

1 package yellow cake mix

½ cup (1 stick) butter, melted

2 cups shredded coconut

1 tablespoon water

1 can (20 ounces) sliced apples

½ cup sugar

½ teaspoon ground cinnamon

1 cup sour cream

2 egg yolks

1. Preheat oven to 350°F. Lightly oil a 10- by 14-inch baking dish.

2. In a large bowl, thoroughly combine cake mix, butter, coconut, and water.

3. Spoon the mixture into the baking dish. Bake for 10 to 12 minutes and remove from the oven.

4. Drain the apple slices and spread evenly over the cooked cake crust. Combine sugar and cinnamon. Reserve 1 tablespoon for the topping. Sprinkle over the apple slices.

5. In a small bowl, beat together the sour cream and egg yolks; drizzle evenly over the apple slices.

6. Sprinkle the reserved 1 tablespoon sugar and cinnamon mixture over the top. Return to the oven and bake for 20 minutes, until top is lightly browned. Serve warm or at room temperature.

Yield: 8 servings

ORCHARD PROFILE

Hollabaugh Brothers Orchards

Owners: Hollabaugh Family

Kay and Brad Hollabaugh are part of the Hollabaugh Brothers Orchards; they grow apples, peaches, plums and apricots. Brad, the secretary of Hollabaugh Bros., Inc., received the American Fruit Grower Magazine's prestigious "Apple Grower of the Year" award for the year 2000. The award annually honors a distinguished apple grower in the United States. One of the criteria for the award is "a history of positive contributions to the industry," says Laurie Sanders, editor of the magazine.

Kay Hollabaugh says that it was an unexpected but sweet reward for all the hard work they put into the orchard.

"There is something very special about seeing the first fruits to come from the tree, whether it's apricots or plums, peaches or apples. The nice thing about working on a farm is that just as things are getting to the point where you are sick of doing them, it's time to do something else. Spring bedding plants arrive and then leave, peaches come and go, apples are here and then gone, and soon it starts all over again with winter pruning and spring planting. I love being a participant in the stewardship of the land," says Kay.

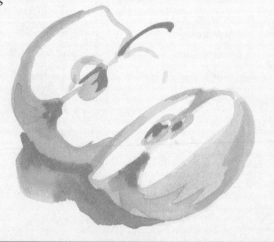

Kay Hollabaugh's Apple Nut Cake

Busy with a farm and a young family, Kay also spends a lot of time in the kitchen. This apple nut cake is her favorite apple dessert because it's rich, sweet, delicious, and loaded with fresh apples!

2 cups sugar

1 cup vegetable oil

3 eggs

3 cups flour

1 teaspoon baking soda

½ teaspoon salt

6 medium apples (Nittany or Golden Delicious), cored, peeled, and diced

1 cup chopped nuts

2 teaspoons vanilla extract

TOPPING

1 cup brown sugar

½ cup (1 stick) butter

¼ cup milk

1. Preheat oven to 350°F. Lightly oil or spray a 9- by 13-inch baking dish.

2. Mix sugar, oil, and eggs in a large bowl; beat well.

3. Add flour, baking soda, salt, apples, nuts, and vanilla and beat just until combined thoroughly.

4. Scrape batter into the prepared baking dish. Bake for 1 hour.

5. TO MAKE THE TOPPING, boil together the brown sugar, butter, and milk for 2½ minutes. Remove from heat.

6. Remove the cake from the oven, and immediately poke the tines of a fork down through the cake (about 15 jabs all around the cake), and pour the topping over the hot cake. Serve warm or let cool.

Yield: 8 to 12 servings

Chocolate Applesauce Cake

This is a very moist, rich cake, and if the applesauce is too liquid, it will be puddinglike. So if you are using homemade applesauce make sure it's more apple than liquid. Otherwise, reduce the applesauce by ½ cup.

¼ cup graham cracker crumbs

8 ounces semisweet chocolate

1½ cups dark brown sugar

1 cup (2 sticks) butter, softened

4 eggs

1½ cups sifted all-purpose flour

2 tablespoons unsweetened cocoa powder

2 teaspoons baking powder

1 teaspoon baking soda

½ teaspoon ground cinnamon

1½ cups applesauce

1. Grease a 9-inch springform pan and dust with the graham cracker crumbs.

2. Place the chocolate in a small ovenproof bowl and place in the oven. Turn the oven thermostat to 350°F and remove the chocolate after 10 minutes to finish melting in the hot bowl.

3. Cream the sugar and butter until fluffy. Add the eggs, one at a time; beat until combined. Beat in the chocolate.

4. Sift together the flour, cocoa, baking powder, baking soda, and cinnamon.

5. Stir approximately ½ cup of the flour mixture and ½ cup of the applesauce into the butter mixture. Continue to combine the ingredients until all have been mixed into the batter.

6. Spoon the batter into the prepared pan and bake for 1 hour 10 minutes, or until a skewer inserted into the center comes out clean.

7. Let cool for 10 minutes in the pan on a wire rack. The cake will shrink. Use a knife to loosen the cake before releasing the spring and lifting the sides from the bottom of the pan. Cool completely before serving.

Yield: 20 servings

Apple Lemon Cake

*My Aunty Kath serves one of the best afternoon teas and always
includes lemon cake. Because she lives in Wales, I don't get to enjoy
the one she makes very often. Luckily, she gave me the recipe.*

3 medium apples
(Winesap, Braeburn,
Macoun)

1 medium lemon

1 cup (2 sticks) butter,
melted

½ cup vegetable oil

3 eggs

2 cups sugar

3 cups sifted all-purpose
flour

1 teaspoon baking powder

1 teaspoon baking soda

1 cup chopped pecans

GLAZE

1 cup confectioners' sugar

2 tablespoons butter,
softened

3 tablespoons lemon juice

1 teaspoon grated lemon
zest

1 tablespoon honey

1. Preheat oven to 350°F and grease and flour a 10-inch tube pan.

2. Peel, core, and chop the apples. Place in a bowl.

3. Grate the lemon zest. Set aside.

4. Squeeze the juice of the lemon over the chopped apple and toss to coat each piece.

5. Pour the butter into a large mixing bowl. Add the oil and beat in the eggs, one at a time. Beat in the sugar and 3 teaspoons of the lemon zest.

6. Sift together the flour, baking powder, and baking soda. Stir into the batter.

7. Fold in the pecans and apples.

8. Pour the batter into the prepared pan and bake for 1 hour 20 minutes, or until a skewer inserted into the middle comes out clean.

9. Remove from the oven; let cool 10 minutes in the pan. Turn onto a wire rack. Prick the top of the cake with the tines of a fork.

10. FOR THE GLAZE, sift the confectioners' sugar into a small bowl and beat in the butter, lemon juice, lemon zest, and honey. Spread over the warm cake.

Yield: 15–20 servings

Applesauce Gingerbread

This is one of my favorite cakes. Depending on the thickness of the applesauce, it is sometimes more puddinglike than it should be. If your applesauce is a little on the thin side, reduce the measurement to ⅔ cup to be sure of a firmer cake.

1 cup (2 sticks) butter

1 cup brown sugar

½ cup molasses

2 eggs

1 cup applesauce

2 cups all-purpose flour

2 teaspoons baking soda

2 teaspoons ground ginger

1 teaspoon ground cinnamon

1. Preheat oven to 350°F. Grease and flour a 9- by 13-inch baking dish.

2. Melt the butter over low heat. Pour into a medium-sized bowl.

3. Beat in the sugar and molasses. Add the eggs, one at a time, and beat.

4. Beat in the applesauce.

5. Sift the flour, baking soda, ginger, and cinnamon into the applesauce mixture and stir well to combine thoroughly.

6. Spoon into the baking dish and bake for 35 minutes, or until a skewer inserted into the middle comes out clean.

7. Remove from the oven and let cool for 5 minutes. Turn onto a wire rack; cool completely.

8. Serve with whipped cream or vanilla ice cream, if desired.

Yield: 18 servings

Apple Kuchen

If you're pressed for time, substitute a cake mix for the flour, sugar, baking powder, and butter. Then add the liquids, apples, and topping.

1¼ cups all-purpose flour

½ cup sugar

1½ teaspoons baking powder

4 tablespoons butter

1 egg

¼ cup apple juice or cider

2 teaspoons vanilla extract

2 large apples (Fuji, Ida Red, Cortland, Rome Beauty)

½ cup pecan halves

GLAZE

4 tablespoons butter

¼ cup honey

1. Preheat oven to 400°F. Grease a 9- by 13-inch baking dish.

2. In a medium-sized bowl, combine the flour, sugar, and baking powder. Cut in the butter with two knives or a pastry blender until the mixture resembles crumbs.

3. Beat together the egg, apple juice, and vanilla. Stir into the crumb mixture.

4. Spread the batter into the prepared dish.

5. Peel, core, and cut the apples into ½-inch slices. Arrange on top of the batter.

6. Dot the apple slices with the pecan halves.

7. FOR THE GLAZE, melt the butter and honey in a small saucepan. Pour over the apples and pecans.

8. Bake for 35 minutes. Serve warm.

Yield: 12 servings

SIMPLE SPICE FROSTING

For a cream-cheese frosting with a special flavor, combine 8 ounces softened cream cheese, 1 stick softened butter, 1 cup confectioners' sugar, 2 tablespoons apple juice, and 1 teaspoon ground cinnamon in a large bowl and beat until fluffy. Spread on top of fruit breads and cakes.

Oatmeal Apple Cupcakes

As cupcakes go, these little morsels are pretty nutritious.
So much so, that they can double as breakfast muffins.

½ cup (1 stick) butter, softened

½ cup brown sugar

½ cup honey

1 cup applesauce

2 eggs

1 cup sifted all-purpose flour

1 cup old-fashioned rolled oats

½ cup whole-wheat flour

1½ teaspoons baking powder

1 teaspoon ground allspice

1 teaspoon baking soda

APPLE GLAZE (OPTIONAL)

2 teaspoons cornstarch

½ cup apple juice or cider

½ cup frozen apple juice concentrate

½ teaspoon ground cinnamon

¼ cup confectioners' sugar (optional)

1. Preheat oven to 375°F. Line 24 muffin cups with paper liners.

2. In a medium-sized bowl, cream together the butter and brown sugar. Beat in the honey, applesauce, and eggs.

3. Mix together the flours, oats, baking powder, allspice, and baking soda. Stir into the applesauce mixture.

4. Fill the paper cups half full with the batter. Bake for 20 minutes, or until a skewer inserted into the center of a cupcake comes out clean. Remove from the muffin pans and cool on wire racks. Frost with Apple Glaze, if desired.

5. FOR THE APPLE GLAZE, mix the cornstarch with a drop of the apple juice to make a smooth paste. Gradually stir into the rest of the juice in a small saucepan.

6. Cook over low heat, stirring constantly, until thick and smooth. Stir in the apple juice concentrate and cinnamon. Remove from the heat. For a sweeter glaze, beat in the confectioners' sugar, if desired.

7. Cool slightly and spoon over the cupcakes or a warm cake.

Yield: 24 cupcakes

IF YOU WERE TO SET OUT to collect recipes for apple desserts, you could quite easily go berserk. In my opinion, only an encyclopedia can do justice to all the apple desserts in creation. After trying out more than I care to remember, I am still partial to the old-fashioned favorites — the crisps, crumbles, cobblers, and puddings. Although, when I'm in the mood for something a little fancier, I make crêpes or a fragrant soufflé.

APPLE
Desserts

Caramel Toffee Apples

These apple confections are not only for children at Halloween. Make them for any occasion or party, and you'll find that they appeal to adults as well.

10–12 small apples (Pink Lady, McIntosh, Honeycrisp, Ginger Gold, Cameo)

10–12 wooden craft sticks

1 cup chopped nuts (pecans, walnuts, or roasted peanuts), toasted

½ cup chocolate chips, chopped

½ cup (1 stick) butter

2 cups brown sugar

1 can (14 ounces) sweetened condensed milk

1 cup dark corn syrup

2 teaspoons vanilla extract

1 teaspoon ground cinnamon

1. Wash and dry the apples well. Remove the stem of each apple, and make a small slit in the top with a sharp narrow knife; insert a craft stick into the slit.

2. Combine the nuts and the chocolate chips on a large piece of wax paper; set aside on a work surface. Place another sheet of wax paper adjacent to the nut mixture.

3. Melt the butter in a 2- to 3-quart pan over low heat. Stir in the sugar, milk, and corn syrup. Cook the mixture over medium heat, stirring regularly, until it reaches 245°F (the hard ball stage) on a candy thermometer. Remove the pan from the heat and stir in the vanilla and cinnamon.

4. Dip the apples into the hot mixture, swirling until covered, or using a spatula or spoon to spread the coating evenly.

5. While the coating is still hot, roll the apples in the nut and chocolate mixture. Stand the coated apples on the sheet of wax paper to allow the coating to cool and set, about 20 minutes.

Yield: 10 to 12 apples

Apple Molasses Cookies

Anything that tastes of molasses and ginger takes me right back to childhood. Whereas chocolate cookies and bars were not considered the best fare for school snacks, I was given unlimited freedom to eat ginger-snaps. My mother thought they were healthful, because they contained molasses, a source of iron.

3 cups sifted all-purpose flour

1½ teaspoons ground ginger

1 teaspoon baking soda

½ teaspoon ground nutmeg

1 cup (2 sticks) butter, softened

1 cup brown sugar

2 eggs

½ cup molasses

¼ cup apple juice or cider

1. In a medium-sized bowl, mix together the flour, ginger, baking soda, and nutmeg.

2. In a large bowl, cream together the butter and sugar. Add the eggs and beat until combined.

3. Beat in the molasses and apple juice.

4. Stir in the flour mixture and beat until smooth.

5. Cover and refrigerate for approximately 1 hour.

6. Preheat oven to 375°F. Grease two large baking sheets.

7. Using a tablespoon, drop the dough 2 inches apart onto the baking sheets. Bake for 10 minutes or until the cookies are lightly browned around the edges. Remove from the trays and cool on wire racks.

Yield: Approximately 40 cookies

NATIONAL APPLE MONTH

October positively sings of apples and autumn. No wonder that the apple connoisseurs have turned it into National Apple Month. A visit to the orchards at this time of year is a wonderful assault on the senses. The soft autumn days are redolent with the winy fragrance of ripe fruit and the woody smell of smoke that lingers in the damp air.

Apple Cinnamon Squares

The combination of apples and cinnamon is one of the all-time greats. If you like cinnamon, this recipe is bursting with it.

½ cup (1 stick) plus
    2 tablespoons butter

¾ cup brown sugar

2 eggs

2 teaspoons vanilla extract

⅓ cup whole-wheat flour

⅔ cup sifted all-purpose flour

2 tablespoons plus 1½
    teaspoons ground
    cinnamon

1 teaspoon baking powder

½ teaspoon baking soda

1 large apple (Rome Beauty,
    Jonagold, Fuji)

½ cup raisins or dried
    cranberries

½ cup granulated sugar

1. Preheat oven to 350°F. Grease and flour an 8-inch-square baking dish.

2. Melt ½ cup of the butter in a 2½-quart saucepan. Remove from the heat and stir in the brown sugar.

3. Beat in the eggs, one at a time. Add the vanilla.

4. Stir in the whole-wheat flour. Sift in the all-purpose flour, 1½ teaspoons of the cinnamon, baking powder, and baking soda. Stir together.

5. Peel, core, and dice the apple. Add to the batter with the raisins and stir to combine. Pour into the baking dish.

6. Mix the remaining 2 tablespoons cinnamon and the granulated sugar. Sprinkle over the top of the batter.

7. Melt the remaining 2 tablespoons butter and drizzle over the sugar and cinnamon.

8. Bake for 30 minutes, or until a skewer inserted into the center comes out clean. Remove and cool in the pan on a wire rack. When cool, slice into squares.

Yield: 16 squares

Apple and Date Squares

If desired, substitute other dried fruits — such as raisins, cranberries, blueberries, or cherries — for the dates. Or use a cup of mixed fruits.

1 cup brown sugar

½ cup (1 stick) butter, softened

2 eggs

1 cup sifted all-purpose flour

1 teaspoon ground cinnamon

½ teaspoon baking powder

½ teaspoon baking soda

¼ teaspoon ground cloves

¼ teaspoon ground nutmeg

1 large apple (Mutsu/Crispin, Fuji, Jonathan, Winesap)

1 cup chopped dates

½ cup chopped walnuts

1. Preheat oven to 350°F. Grease and flour an 8-inch-square baking dish.

2. In a medium-sized bowl, cream together the sugar and butter until fluffy.

3. Beat in the eggs, one at a time.

4. Sift in the flour, cinnamon, baking powder, baking soda, cloves, and nutmeg. Stir to combine.

5. Peel, core, and chop the apple. Stir the apples, dates, and walnuts into the batter. Pour into the prepared baking dish.

6. Bake for 30 minutes, or until a skewer inserted into the center comes out clean. Cool in the pan on a wire rack. When cool, slice into squares.

Yield: 16 squares

Sweet Applesauce

A dessert applesauce, this is delicious all on its own.

10 medium apples (any kind except Red Delicious or summer-harvested apples such as Lodi, Tydeman Red, Puritan)

3 tablespoons apple juice or cider

⅓ cup honey or ½ cup brown sugar

3 tablespoons butter

½ teaspoon ground cinnamon

½ teaspoon ground ginger

1. Peel, core, and quarter the apples. Place in a large saucepan with the apple juice.

2. Cover the pot and simmer for approximately 30 minutes, or until the apples are tender. Purée in a blender or food processor.

3. Stir the honey, butter, cinnamon, and ginger into the warm apple purée.

Yield: About 5½ cups

NUTRITIVE VALUE
OF A 2¾-INCH, 138-GRAM RAW APPLE WITH SKIN*

Water	83.93 percent	Potassium	158.7 milligrams
Calories	81	Vitamin A	73.14 International Units
Protein	0.262 gram		
Fat	0.8 gram	Vitamin B$_6$	0.066 milligram
Carbohydrates	21.045 grams	Thiamin	0.023 milligram
Calcium	9.66 milligrams	Riboflavin	0.019 milligram
Phosphorus	9.66 milligrams	Niacin	0.106 milligram
Iron	0.248 milligram	Vitamin C (ascorbic acid)	7.866 milligrams
Sodium	0.00		

*There are about three 2¾-inch apples in a pound. Source: U.S.D.A. Nutrient Database for Standard Reference, Release 13 (November 1999)

Nancy Black's School Brownies

When my daughter Wendy was in first grade (she graduated from college last year!), she brought home one of her teacher's brownies in her lunch box. It was so wonderful, I asked for the recipe and still use it. Here it is.

1 cup sugar

½ cup (1 stick) butter, at room temperature

1 egg

1 cup sifted all-purpose flour

1½ teaspoons baking powder

½ teaspoon baking soda

½ teaspoon ground cinnamon

¼ teaspoon ground nutmeg

1 large apple (Rome Beauty, Fuji, Mutsu/Crispin, Jonagold)

¾ cup chopped walnuts

1 teaspoon vanilla extract

1. Preheat oven to 350°F. Grease and flour an 8-inch-square baking dish.

2. Cream together the sugar and butter in a medium-sized bowl.

3. Beat in the egg.

4. In another bowl, mix the flour, baking powder, baking soda, cinnamon, and nutmeg. Stir into the batter.

5. Peel, core, and dice the apple. Add to the batter with the walnuts and vanilla. Stir to combine.

6. Pour into the baking dish and bake for 30 minutes, or until a skewer inserted into the center comes out clean. Cool in the pan on a wire rack. Slice into squares.

Yield: 16 servings

Maple Apple Crisp

So good and so easy, there's no excuse not to make dessert from scratch — especially if you substitute apple-pie filling for fresh apple slices because you'll knock almost 10 minutes off the preparation.

1   cup granola

½   cup old-fashioned rolled oats

½   cup dark brown sugar

½   cup chopped walnuts or pecans

1   teaspoon ground cinnamon

½   cup (1 stick) butter

4   large apples (Winesap, Ida Red, Northern Spy, Braeburn)

⅓   cup pure maple syrup

1   tablespoon lemon juice

1. Preheat oven to 400°F. Grease a deep 2-quart baking dish.

2. In a medium-sized bowl, combine the granola, oats, sugar, walnuts, and cinnamon. Using your fingers, blend the butter into the mixture.

3. Peel, core, and cut the apples into ¼-inch slices. Place in the baking dish and sprinkle with the maple syrup and lemon juice.

4. Cover completely with the granola mixture and bake for 40 minutes, or until the apples are tender when pierced. Serve warm with ice cream, if desired.

Yield: 6–8 servings

Apple Blackberry Crisp

There are pounds of blackberries for the picking on the hills behind my mother's house in Argyll, Scotland. Although most are used for jam and jelly making, some find their way into dessert dishes such as this delectable one.

4 large apples (Rome Beauty, Winesap, Ida Red)

1½–2 cups blackberries

½ cup granulated sugar

1 cup plus 2 tablespoons all-purpose flour

½ cup brown sugar

1 teaspoon cinnamon

½ cup (1 stick) butter

1. Preheat oven to 400°F and grease a deep 2-quart casserole dish.

2. Peel, core, and cut the apples into ¼-inch slices. Cook over low heat for 10 minutes. Place in the baking dish, and add the blackberries.

3. Combine the granulated sugar and 2 tablespoons of the flour. Mix into the apple slices and blackberries.

4. In a medium-sized bowl, mix together the remaining 1 cup flour, brown sugar, and cinnamon. Cut in the butter until the mixture resembles coarse crumbs.

5. Sprinkle over the apple filling and bake for 30 minutes, or until the crumbs are golden brown. Serve warm with English Custard Sauce (page 152) or heavy cream.

Yield: 8 servings

Tom Carrolan's Apple Crisp

When I lived in Westchester County, New York, Tom and I belonged to Bedford Audubon's birding group. After sampling some of my recipes on a number of our outings, he finally gave me his recipe for "the best apple crisp." Tom serves his crisp warm with heavy cream. It is sinfully delicious.

9–10   medium apples (Northern Spy)
2   tablespoons honey
¼   cup apple juice or cider
1   cup brown sugar
¾   cup all-purpose flour
½   teaspoon ground cinnamon
½   teaspoon ground nutmeg
½   cup (1 stick) butter

1. Preheat oven to 350°F and grease a 2-quart casserole dish.

2. Peel, core, and thinly slice the apples. Place in the dish, drizzle with honey, and add the apple juice.

3. Mix the sugar, flour, cinnamon, and nutmeg in a small bowl. Cut in the butter with two knives or a pastry blender until the mixture resembles coarse crumbs. Sprinkle over the apples.

4. Cover the casserole dish with aluminum foil and bake for 30 minutes. Remove the foil and bake for 30 minutes longer.

Yield: 8–10 servings

Apple Rhubarb Slump

"Slump" is a New England name for a fruit dessert topped with a sweet dumpling mixture. On Cape Cod, traditionalists call slumps "grunts." In other parts of the country, they fall under the heading of "cobblers." No matter what they're called, they all taste good.

4 medium apples (McIntosh, Golden Delicious)

2 cups rhubarb, cut into 1-inch pieces

¾ cup plus 2 tablespoons sugar

½ teaspoon ground cinnamon

½ teaspoon ground ginger

¼ teaspoon ground cloves

1 cup all-purpose flour

1½ teaspoons baking powder

3 tablespoons butter

½ cup milk

2 teaspoons vanilla extract

1. Preheat oven to 400°F; grease a 2-quart baking dish.

2. Peel, core, and slice the apples into ½-inch pieces. Place in a saucepan and add the rhubarb, ¾ cup of the sugar, cinnamon, ginger, and cloves. Cover the dish and cook over low heat for about 10 minutes, stirring once or twice, until the apple slices are tender but not falling apart.

3. In a medium-sized bowl, sift the flour and baking powder. Stir in the remaining 2 tablespoons sugar. Cut in the butter until the mixture resembles crumbs.

4. Stir the milk and vanilla into the crumb mixture until just blended. Do not overmix.

5. Pour the hot apple-rhubarb mixture into the greased dish and spoon the dough in dollops over the top.

6. Bake for 25–30 minutes, until golden. Serve warm with English Custard Sauce (page 152) or whipped cream.

Yield: 8 servings

Apple Apricot Cobbler

A cobbler topping is somewhere between cake and biscuit batter, so it develops a slightly crusty texture. This apple apricot flavor is one of my favorites, especially with a bright touch of orange juice.

1 cup dried apricots

½ cup orange juice

5 large apples (Jonagold, Fuji, Braeburn, Gala, or a mix of several)

½ cup plus 1 tablespoon brown sugar

½ teaspoon ground allspice

¼ teaspoon ground cloves

¼ teaspoon ground ginger

¾ cup (1½ sticks) butter, softened

¾ cup granulated sugar

2 eggs

1 tablespoon vanilla extract

1½ cups sifted all-purpose flour

2 teaspoons baking powder

1. Halve the apricots, place in a medium-sized saucepan, and cover with the orange juice.

2. Preheat oven to 375°F. Grease a 2- or 2½-quart baking dish.

3. Peel, core, and cut the apples into ¼-inch slices. Add to the apricots along with ½ cup of the brown sugar, the allspice, cloves, and ginger. Mix well and simmer for 10 minutes.

4. In a medium-sized bowl, beat the butter and granulated sugar until fluffy. Beat in the eggs, one at a time. Stir in the vanilla.

5. Stir the flour and baking powder into the bowl and beat until blended.

6. Put the apple mixture into the baking dish and cover with the batter. Sprinkle the top with the remaining 1 tablespoon brown sugar.

7. Bake for 40 minutes, or until the crust is golden brown.

Yield: 8 servings

Barbara Mullin's Apple Cobbler

*Working every day at Haight's Orchard in Croton Falls, New York,
Barbara didn't have much time for fancy cooking. Her recipe for
apple cobbler is simple and superb.*

6 large apples (Jonathan)
1 cup flour
½ cup brown sugar
½ cup granulated sugar
1 teaspoon baking powder
1 teaspoon ground cinnamon
1 egg
5⅓ tablespoons butter

1. Preheat oven to 350°F and grease a 2-quart baking dish.

2. Peel, core, and cut the apples into ¼-inch slices.

3. In a medium-sized bowl, mix the flour, brown sugar, granulated sugar, baking powder, and cinnamon. Beat the egg lightly and stir into the sugar mixture. Spoon on top of the sliced apples.

4. Melt the butter in a small pan and drizzle over the batter.

5. Bake for 45 minutes.

Yield: 8 servings

JOHNNY APPLESEED

The most famous apple seed sower was John Chapman, or Johnny Appleseed as everyone came to know him. Born in Massachusetts in 1774, he left home at an early age to follow the pioneers to the new frontiers with the intention of teaching the Bible and planting apple nurseries from seeds and cuttings. He accomplished this mission, and when he died in Indiana in 1854, he was making his customary rounds of his many apple trees.

Apple Brown Betty

Brown Betty calls for alternate layers of bread and apples. On one of her visits home, my daughter Wendy made some lemon cupcakes, ate one, and then departed. What to do with the leftover cupcakes? I cut them into cubes and layered them in an Apple Brown Betty. It was so delicious I'll do the same again. This recipe is based on the traditional layers of bread.

¾ cup brown sugar

1 teaspoon ground cinnamon

½ teaspoon ground nutmeg

¼ teaspoon ground cloves

6 slices bread or 3 cups cake cubes

½ cup (1 stick) butter

3 tablespoons lemon juice

4 large apples (Rome Beauty, Winesap, Cortland, Jonathan)

¼ cup apple juice or cider

1. Preheat oven to 350°F and grease a 2-quart baking dish.

2. In a large bowl, mix the sugar, cinnamon, nutmeg, and cloves. Crumble in the bread.

3. Melt the butter, add the lemon juice, and stir into the crumbled-bread mixture.

4. Peel, core, and thinly slice the apples.

5. Cover the bottom of the baking dish with a layer of the crumbs (about one-third of the mixture), add half the apples, a layer of crumbs, the rest of the apples, and the remaining crumbs.

6. Pour the apple juice over the top, cover with aluminum foil, and bake for 30 minutes. Remove the cover and bake for 20 minutes longer. Serve warm.

Yield: 8 servings

English Apple Crumble

This is my mother's basic recipe for fruit crumble.
It's like a crisp, but not as rich. She uses it with apples, rhubarb,
blackberries, raspberries, gooseberries, and whatever else grows in
her garden. From the old school, Mother likes to use tart
apples in her pies and crumbles.

6 medium tart apples (Granny Smith, Rhode Island Greening, Twenty Ounce)

⅓ plus ¼ cup sugar

juice of ½ lemon

1 teaspoon ground cinnamon

¾ cup all-purpose flour

4 tablespoons butter

additional sugar for sprinkling (optional)

1. Preheat oven to 400°F and grease a 2-quart baking dish.

2. Peel, core, and cut the apples into ½-inch slices. Place in a saucepan with ⅓ cup of the sugar, lemon juice, and cinnamon. Cook over low heat, stirring once or twice, for 10 minutes, or until the apple slices are tender but not falling apart. Spoon into the baking dish.

3. Combine the flour and the remaining ¼ cup sugar in a small bowl. Cut in the butter with a pastry blender or two knives until the mixture is crumbly. Sprinkle on top of the apples. (I like to sprinkle the crumbs with 2 teaspoons sugar.)

4. Bake for 30 minutes, or until golden brown.

Yield: 8 servings

Apple Raisin Crunch

For a really decadent crunch, crisp, or cobbler, drizzle a few table-spoons of melted butter over the top before popping it into the oven.

4   medium apples (Granny Smith, Newtown Pippin, Northern Spy, Braeburn)

1   cup golden raisins

¼   cup orange juice

1   cup plus 2 tablespoons brown sugar

1   teaspoon ground allspice

1   teaspoon grated orange zest

1   cup all-purpose flour

¾   cup old-fashioned rolled oats

½   teaspoon ground cinnamon

½   cup (1 stick) butter

1. Preheat oven to 400°F and grease a 2-quart baking dish.

2. Peel, core, and slice the apples into ¼-inch pieces.

3. In the baking dish, combine the apples with the raisins, orange juice, 2 tablespoons of the sugar, allspice, and orange zest.

4. In a medium-sized bowl, mix the flour, the remaining 1 cup sugar, oats, and cinnamon. Cut in the butter with a pastry blender or two knives until the mixture is crumbly. Sprinkle on top of the apples and raisins.

5. Bake for 30 minutes, or until the top is golden.

Yield: 8 servings

APPLES AND LOVE

It's said that the game of bobbing for apples began as a Celtic New Year's tradition for trying to determine one's future spouse.

Johnny Appleseed Squares

This is another fast and easy recipe from the files of the U.S. Apple Association. It appeals to me because I love sweetened condensed milk, and because it can be thrown together in the blink of an eye. You don't need to peel the apples if they have thin skins.

5 medium apples (a mix of your favorites), peeled, if desired, cored, and sliced (about 6 cups)

1 can (14 ounces) sweetened, condensed milk

1 teaspoon ground cinnamon

1½ cups biscuit baking mix

½ cup (1 stick) plus 2 tablespoons cold butter

½ cup firmly packed brown sugar

½ cup chopped walnuts or pecans

1. Preheat oven to 325°F. Lightly oil (or use a cooking oil spray) a 9-inch-square baking dish.

2. Combine the apples with the condensed milk and cinnamon in a medium-sized bowl.

3. Measure 1 cup of the biscuit mix into a medium-sized bowl and cut in ½ cup of the butter with two knives or a pastry blender until it resembles large crumbs.

4. Stir in the apple mixture and spoon the batter into the baking dish.

5. In a small bowl, combine the remaining ½ cup biscuit mix with the sugar and cut in the remaining 2 tablespoons of cold butter until crumbs form. Stir in the nuts.

6. Sprinkle the nut mixture evenly over the apple batter and bake for 50–60 minutes, until a skewer inserted into the center comes out clean.

7. Serve warm with vanilla yogurt or ice cream.

Yield: 8 servings

Sherried Apple Crêpes

*The whipped cream folded into the filling makes these very
special party crêpes. However, I actually prefer whipped dairy
topping because it is not as rich as real cream.*

 4 small apples (McIntosh,
    Golden Delicious)

¼ cup apricot jam

¼ cup sugar

 3 tablespoons golden raisins

 2 tablespoons slivered
    blanched almonds

 1 tablespoon apple juice or
    water

½ teaspoon ground cinnamon

½ teaspoon ground nutmeg

 8 crêpes (pages 20–21)

 1 cup heavy cream

 2 tablespoons confectioners'
    sugar

 1 tablespoon sherry

1. Peel, core, and thinly slice the apples. Place in a pan with the jam, sugar, raisins, almonds, apple juice, cinnamon, and nutmeg. Mix together.

2. Simmer gently, stirring occasionally, for 10–15 minutes, or until the apples are soft and the mixture is thick. Let cool.

3. Make the crêpes following the dessert variation of the basic recipe on pages 20–21.

4. Whip the cream until thickened, stir in the confectioners' sugar and sherry, and continue beating until soft peaks form.

5. Fold half of the whipped cream into the apple mixture. Spread the filling over the crêpes, fold in half, then in half again to form triangles. Top each crêpe with a spoonful of remaining whipped cream.

Yield: 8 servings

Meringue-Topped Baked Apples

*This dessert has always been a favorite with my daughter,
Wendy. Not one for cakes, she loves any meringue dessert.
Because I didn't make this recipe regularly, it encouraged her
to start baking at a very early age.*

4   medium apples (Jonathan,
      Ida Red, Braeburn)

¼   cup apple juice or cider

¼   cup honey

2   tablespoons butter

½   teaspoon ground cinnamon

½   teaspoon ground nutmeg

3   egg whites, at room
      temperature

¼   teaspoon cream of tartar

¼   cup sugar

1. Preheat oven to 350°F. Grease a 9- by 13-inch baking dish.

2. Core the apples. Cut into halves and arrange, cut side up, in the dish.

3. Combine the apple juice, honey, butter, cinnamon, and nutmeg in a small saucepan. Heat and stir until the butter has melted. Pour over the apples.

4. Cover with aluminum foil and bake for 15 minutes. Remove the foil and bake for 15 minutes longer, or until tender.

5. In a wide bowl, beat the egg whites with the cream of tartar until foamy. Add the sugar, 2 tablespoons at a time, and continue beating until peaks form.

6. Spoon the meringue over each warm apple half and bake for 10 minutes, or until the meringue is tinged golden brown. Serve warm.

Yield: 8 servings

Baked Apple Slices

*When you want a very simple dessert that is neither heavy nor rich,
this is a good one to choose. Moreover, you can eat the leftovers for
breakfast or serve them as a side dish at dinner.*

6 large apples (Mutsu/Crispin, Jonagold, Ida Red, Rome Beauty)

½ cup brown sugar or maple sugar

¼ cup sifted all-purpose flour

1 teaspoon ground cinnamon

¼ teaspoon ground cloves

¼ teaspoon ground ginger

4 tablespoons butter

¼ cup apple juice or cider

1. Preheat oven to 350°F. Grease a large baking dish.

2. Core the apples. Cut each into 6 wedges and arrange in a single layer in the dish.

3. Mix the sugar, flour, cinnamon, cloves, and ginger. Sprinkle over the apples.

4. Melt the butter and mix with the apple juice. Pour over the top and toss to combine. Cover the dish with aluminum foil.

5. Bake for 20 minutes. Uncover and bake for 15 minutes longer. Serve warm.

Yield: 6–8 servings

Vanilla Soufflé

Not your usual soufflé, this uses caramelized apple slices to create a sauce.

4 medium apples (Gala, Braeburn, Empire, Golden Delicious)

7 tablespoons butter

⅓ plus ¼ cup sugar

1 teaspoon ground cinnamon

⅔ cup milk

3 tablespoons sifted all-purpose flour

5 eggs, at room temperature and separated

1 tablespoon vanilla extract

¼ teaspoon cream of tartar

1 tablespoon confectioner's sugar (optional)

1. Preheat oven to 400°F. Grease a 1½-quart baking dish.

2. Peel, core, and cut the apples into ½-inch slices. In a skillet, melt 4 tablespoons of the butter and sauté the apples for 5 minutes over medium heat.

3. Mix ⅓ cup of the sugar with the cinnamon. Sprinkle over the apples; stir. Sauté the apples until they begin to caramelize, about 10 minutes. The mixture will be syrupy and the apples tender. Remove from heat; spoon into the baking dish.

4. Place the milk and the remaining 3 tablespoons butter in a small saucepan; bring almost to a boil. Remove from heat.

5. Put the remaining ¼ cup sugar and flour into a bowl.

6. In a small bowl, beat the egg yolks and vanilla. Pour into the sugar and flour and blend. Pour in the milk mixture and blend or beat for 30 seconds. Return the mixture to the pan and cook over low heat, stirring constantly, for 2 minutes, or until thickened. Do not overcook, or the eggs will scramble.

7. Using a wire whip or an electric beater, beat the egg whites in a large bowl with the cream of tartar until they form smooth, shiny peaks. Stir one-third into the egg yolk mixture, then carefully and quickly fold in the rest.

8. Spoon the soufflé over the apple base and place in the preheated oven. Bake 15 minutes. Remove and serve immediately. Sprinkle with the confectioners' sugar, if desired.

Yield: 8 servings

Apple-Cinnamon Soufflé

This is a very easy soufflé to make. For an adult dessert, reduce the milk by 2 tablespoons and replace with applejack or Calvados.

¾ cup milk

3 tablespoons butter

¼ cup sugar

3 tablespoons sifted all-purpose flour

2 teaspoons ground cinnamon

5 eggs, at room temperature and separated

1 cup applesauce

¼ teaspoon cream of tartar

1. Preheat oven to 375°F. Grease a 1-quart soufflé dish. Cut a piece of aluminum foil long enough to go around the outside of the dish and wide enough to extend 3 inches above the dish. Grease the inside of the foil, then tie or pin in place.

2. Put the milk and butter into a small saucepan and bring almost to a boil. Remove from the heat.

3. Measure the sugar, flour, and cinnamon into a bowl or blender. Add the egg yolks. Beat or blend the yolks and flour. Pour in the milk mixture. Beat or blend for 30 seconds. Return to the pan and cook over low heat, stirring continuously, for 2 minutes, or until the mixture thickens.

4. Mix in the applesauce.

5. Using a wire whip or an electric mixer, beat the egg whites in a large bowl with the cream of tartar until they form smooth, shiny peaks. Stir a third into the soufflé base, then carefully and quickly fold in the rest until it is evenly distributed, but not deflated.

6. Pour into the prepared soufflé dish and bake for 35–40 minutes. Gently remove the collar and serve immediately.

Yield: 4 servings

Apple Sorbet

A lovely, light dessert to serve after a heavy meal, apple sorbet is also refreshing as a palate cleanser between courses at a fancy dinner.

2 cups apple juice or cider

2 cups applesauce

¼ cup honey

1 teaspoon ground ginger or ground cinnamon

1. Combine all the ingredients in a medium-sized bowl, blender, or food processor, and blend. Chill for 1 hour.

2. Pour into an ice-cream machine and follow the manufacturer's directions for freezing ice cream. Or pour into a shallow dish and place in the freezer for about 1 hour. Then beat the mixture, cover with aluminum foil, and freeze until firm.

Yield: 1 quart

Apple Fool

Another classic English sweet, fool is a cloud of whipped cream and fruit. It is traditionally made with gooseberries, but other fruits are often used with splendid results.

1 cup heavy cream

2 tablespoons confectioners' sugar

2 cups applesauce

½ teaspoon ground cinnamon

1. Pour the cream into a medium-sized bowl. Add the sugar and beat until stiff.

2. Fold in the applesauce.

3. Spoon into individual dessert dishes, if desired, and sprinkle the tops with the cinnamon.

Yield: 6–8 servings

Apple Sponge Pudding

In Britain, in many regions, dessert is referred to as the "sweet" or the "pudding." Ever since I can remember, we called it pudding. This is not surprising, because many of our desserts were, in fact, sponge or suet puddings containing fruits or preserves. Apple Sponge is one of the classics.

3 medium apples (Golden Delicious, Ida Red, Empire)

⅓ cup honey or maple syrup

1 cup (2 sticks) butter, softened

1 cup granulated sugar

4 eggs

3 tablespoons lemon juice

2 cups sifted all-purpose flour

2 teaspoons baking powder

½ teaspoon baking soda

2 tablespoons brown sugar

1 teaspoon grated lemon zest

½ teaspoon ground cinnamon

1. Preheat oven to 350°F. Grease a 1½- or 2-quart deep baking dish.

2. Peel, core, and cut the apples into ¼-inch slices and place in the dish.

3. Drizzle the honey over the apples.

4. In a large mixing bowl, cream the butter and granulated sugar until light and fluffy.

5. Beat in the eggs, one at a time, then the lemon juice.

6. Stir in the flour, baking powder, and baking soda. Pour the mixture over the apples and smooth the top.

7. Combine the brown sugar, lemon zest, and cinnamon. Sprinkle over the pudding.

8. Bake for 50–60 minutes, until a skewer inserted into the center comes out clean. Serve warm with English Custard Sauce (page 152) heavy cream, or whipped cream.

Yield: 6–8 servings

Microwave Apple Bread Pudding

I grew up eating steamed puddings made from cake batter or day-old bread. They were dense but amazingly light and usually flavored with fruit.

2 cups milk (skim, low-fat, or whole milk)

2 medium apples (Empire, Golden Delicious, Granny Smith, Braeburn), cored and chopped

4 large slices bread, cut or torn into 1-inch pieces

½ cup chopped walnuts or pecans

2 extra large eggs

⅓ cup brown sugar

1 teaspoon vanilla extract

½ teaspoon ground cinnamon

Note: To bake in a traditional oven, preheat to 400°F. Set the uncovered dish in a large baking pan. Add boiling water to come 1 inch up the sides of the dish. Bake for 25 minutes or until puffy and golden.

1. Pour the milk into a 4-cup microwave-safe glass dish and add the chopped apples. Microwave on HIGH for 3–4 minutes, until the milk is sizzling around the sides but not boiling.

2. Combine the bread and walnuts in a 1½-quart soufflé dish.

3. In a small bowl, beat together the eggs, sugar, vanilla, and cinnamon. Slowly whisk ½ cup of the milk into the egg mixture. Stirring continuously, pour the egg mixture slowly into the rest of the milk.

4. Pour the milk mixture into the soufflé dish over the bread and walnuts. Cover the top of the soufflé dish with wax paper.

5. Microwave on HIGH 2 minutes. Remove the dish and stir the mixture gently. Cover with the wax paper.

6. Microwave on MEDIUM 1½ minutes, remove the dish, and stir the edges into the center. Cover with the wax paper.

7. Microwave on MEDIUM 1½ minutes longer. The pudding will not be fully set in the middle.

8. Remove the wax paper; let the pudding sit for 20–30 minutes. Serve it warm or cold.

Yield: 4–6 servings

ORCHARD PROFILE

Breezy Hill Orchard

Owner: Elizabeth Ryan

Elizabeth Ryan, with help from her son, Peter, and a dedicated staff, grows more than 45 varieties of apples. Among their heirloom and antique varieties are Jonathan, Stayman, Golden Russett, King Luscious, and Opalescent. Breezy Hill also grows some of the more modern hybrids, such as Jonagold, Monroe, and Macoun.

In 2000, Ryan expanded her operation to include an orchard in Rhinebeck, New York. It is there that Ryan, who studied pomology and pest management at Cornell University in Ithaca, New York, is creating a showplace for old varieties. This is a state-certified organic farm; instead of fungicides, botanicals, or any other form of pesticides, beneficial insects are released into the orchards. "To encourage the beneficials to stay, we provide shelter and food for them by allowing vegetation to grow under the apple trees," explains Ryan. "The unsprayed apples are pretty funky-looking, but they taste good."

Ryan and her orchard generated interest in predator insects when they collaborated on several experiments with a partnership involving four institutions — Cornell University, the University of Vermont, University of Massachusetts, and Rutgers University — as well as the Rodale Research Center in Pennsylvania. "We planted and managed blocks of apple trees that we were growing organically. In fact, Cornell continues to use our orchards for releasing predator insects," says Ryan. "Also because we are certified organic, Mothers and Others asked us to develop a program called Core Values." Core Values is a stamp of approval that is attached to every apple to indicate to the world that it has been grown in a certified organic ecoprogram.

Breezy Hill Hard Sauce

Elizabeth Ryan likes to offer this hard sauce with apple Betty, crisps, and other baked goodies served warm from the oven.

2 cups confectioners' sugar

½ cup (1 stick) butter, softened

2 tablespoons Calvados

1. Cream together the sugar, butter, and Calvados until light and fluffy. Chill for 2 hours before serving.

Yield: About 2½ cups

Applesauce Brownies

The applesauce adds moistness to these brownies.

½ cup (1 stick) butter

1½ cups brown sugar

1 cup applesauce

2 eggs

2 teaspoons vanilla extract

1¼ cups sifted all-purpose flour

¼ cup unsweetened cocoa powder

1 teaspoon baking powder

½ teaspoon baking soda

½ cup chopped pecans

1. Preheat oven to 350°F. Grease and flour an 8-inch-square baking dish.

2. Melt the butter in a 2½-quart saucepan. Remove from heat and beat in the sugar, applesauce, eggs, and vanilla. Sift in the flour, cocoa, baking powder, and baking soda. Stir to combine. Stir in the pecans.

3. Pour the batter into the prepared baking dish and bake for 25–30 minutes, or until a skewer inserted into the center comes out clean. Cool in the pan on a wire rack. Slice into squares.

Yield: 16 servings

English Custard Sauce

Dinner in Britain, whether at my mother's home or at any of her farming siblings' and relatives', is almost always followed by a sweet dessert. Pies and baked puddings are accompanied with double (clotted) cream or custard, such as this one. You can also serve this sauce with baked apples and any of the crisps and cobblers. While it's usually served warm, it can be refrigerated, and is simply out of this world when cold.

⅓ cup sugar

2 tablespoons cornstarch

3 egg yolks

2 cups milk or light cream

2 teaspoons vanilla extract

1. Combine the sugar and cornstarch, and whisk together with the egg yolks in the top of a double boiler. Whisk until smooth.

2. Heat the milk in a medium-sized saucepan. When it reaches a boil, pour half over the egg mixture, stirring constantly. Add the rest of the milk, then the vanilla.

3. Place the top of the double boiler *over* simmering water (it must not touch the water) and, stirring constantly, cook for 2 minutes, or until the mixture thickens and is smooth.

4. Remove from the heat and pour into a small jug. Serve immediately or cover with wax paper to prevent a skin from forming.

Yield: 2 cups

VARIATION

For a richer custard, whip ½ cup heavy cream until it is thick but not stiff, and stir into the custard. Chill, if desired.

Apricot Apple Dumplings

Apple dumplings can be made quite easily (especially if you use store-bought pastry), yet most people shy away from making them, because they look as though they may be difficult to assemble. Not at all. They go together quite quickly and taste like apple pie, but make a prettier presentation.

6 medium apples (Rome Beauty, Braeburn, Jonathan)

¼ cup apricot preserves

4 tablespoons butter, softened

2 tablespoons brown sugar

pastry for a double piecrust (pages 113–115)

milk

1. Preheat oven to 400°F. Grease a large shallow baking dish.

2. Peel and partially core the apples, leaving approximately ¼ inch of core at the base. Remove the stems and trim the bottoms, if necessary, so that the apples sit level.

3. Beat the preserves, butter, and sugar together. Stuff the mixture into the cores of the apples.

4. Divide the pastry into six pieces and roll out into 6-inch squares approximately ¼-inch thick.

5. Place an apple in the center of each square of dough and bring the four corners of the pastry together. Dab with milk and then seal.

6. Arrange the dumplings in the baking dish (they should not touch one another) and pop into the freezer for 3–5 minutes to chill the pastry.

7. Reduce oven to 375°F. Brush the pastry with milk and bake for 50–60 minutes, or until golden brown. Serve warm with English Custard Sauce (page 152) or vanilla ice cream.

Yield: 6 servings

Caramel Apple Puff Dumplings

This recipe comes from Julia Stewart Daly of the U.S. Apple Association. Julia says her guests are always dazzled when she serves this elegant but deceptively simple dessert.

1 sheet frozen puff pastry

4 medium cooking apples (Golden Delicious or Jonathan)

1 tablespoon brown sugar

1 teaspoon ground cinnamon

1 egg, lightly beaten

1 teaspoon water

1 teaspoon granulated sugar

SAUCE

½ cup prepared caramel sundae topping

⅓ cup toasted chopped pecan halves (optional)

1. Thaw and unfold the pastry as the package directs.

2. Preheat oven to 400°F. On a lightly floured surface, roll the pastry into a 16-inch square and, using a fluted pastry cutter or a kitchen knife, cut into 4 equal squares.

3. Peel and core apples; trim bottoms so that apples sit level. Place one apple in the center of each pastry square. Combine brown sugar and cinnamon; spoon into apples.

4. Beat the egg and water together in a small bowl and moisten the edges of the pastry with the mixture. Bring the pastry up around the apples, pleating or trimming excess pastry as needed, and pinch the edges together to form a seal.

5. Place the dumplings in an ungreased 9- by 13-inch baking dish. Brush them with the egg mixture; sprinkle with the granulated sugar. Bake for about 35 minutes, until golden brown.

6. FOR THE SAUCE, combine the caramel topping and pecan halves, if desired, in a microwave-safe dish. Microwave, uncovered, on HIGH for 30 seconds, until heated through.

7. Spoon the sauce onto each plate and set the dumplings on top or drizzle the sauce over the top. Serve warm.

Yield: 4 servings

PRESERVING
the Apple Harvest

IF YOU'VE BEEN HARVESTING APPLES since August, by the time the end of October rolls around, your family may wish it were a forbidden fruit. This is the time to start preserving.

There are a number of ways to prolong the life of your apples: canning, freezing, and drying. Applesauce and apple slices are a cinch to can or freeze. You may decide to make jams, jellies, and butters or, on the savory side, to try your hand at spicy chutneys and relishes.

If apple pies are a staple in your house, unbaked pies can be frozen and later popped, at a moment's notice, from the freezer (see directions on page 160). I don't like to freeze baked pies; the bottom crust always ends up soggy.

Canning vs. Freezing

Canning and freezing provide long-term storage for apples. Apples will keep for 8–12 months in a freezer before they deteriorate in flavor and texture, especially if they are packed in a sugar or honey syrup. Canned apples and applesauce will keep indefinitely, although it is always best to can only as much as you can eat in a year.

Most people find that they don't have freezer space for frozen apple products, so they prefer to can apples. I prefer canning because I like the convenience of having the apples ready to eat or bake with right out of the jar. Frozen applesauce takes quite a long time to defrost.

Canning Basics

Apple slices, applesauce, and apple preserves can be canned in a boiling-water bath, which consists of a large kettle, a rack that fits inside, and a lid. Apple slices are usually processed for 15 minutes in pints, 20 minutes in quarts. Applesauce is processed for 10 minutes in both pints and quarts. Apple jams and marmalades should also be processed for 10 minutes to ensure a long shelf life.*

Whenever you can fruits or vegetables, you should use special canning jars, which are equipped with flat metal lids and screw bands. The U.S. Department of Agriculture (U.S.D.A.) advises against using bail-top glass lids with a separate rubber seal and metal clamp for canning.

A jar lifter and a wide-necked funnel will make the canning process a lot easier and safer.

After the jars have cooled for 12 hours, check each lid for a proper seal by feeling the depression on the lid. If you find a jar that hasn't sealed (check by turning it upside down to see if it leaks), take a clean jar and a new lid, fill with the mixture, and reprocess for the given time or refrigerate that jar and use within a week or so. Reprocessing applesauce will not affect the texture significantly. Don't bother to reprocess apple slices, however; you will end up with mush instead of slices.

With careful use and handling, Mason jars may be reused many times, requiring only new lids each time.

---

*If you are processing food at an elevation above 1,000 feet, you will need to increase the processing time. Consult your local county Extension agent or contact Cooperative State Research, Education and Extension Service at 202-720-3029 (http://www.reeusda.gov/ on the Internet).

CANNING APPLE SLICES

Canned apple slices are great to use in pies, crêpes, and baked desserts. They are good in fruit salads. However, peeling apples for canning is a laborious chore. When I am working with large quantities of apples, I prefer to can applesauce. Plan to can about 3 medium apples per quart jar.

1. Wash the jars and lids in warm, soapy water and rinse thoroughly. Prepare the lids as the manufacturer directs. Preheat water in your canner.

2. For each quart jar, measure 2 cups water and 1 cup extra fine granulated sugar into a pan and slowly bring to a boil, stirring to dissolve the sugar. Boil the syrup for 5 minutes and remove from the heat.

3. Peel, core, and slice the apples approximately ¼-inch thick. Drop immediately into a bowl containing a gallon of cold water mixed with 2 tablespoons lemon juice.

4. When all the apples are sliced, drain and pack into the quart jars to within ½ inch of the top, without crushing the slices.

5. Return the syrup to a rolling boil and pour over the packed slices, again leaving ½ inch of headroom. Run a rubber spatula or a chopstick around the inside of the jars to release air bubbles. Wipe the rims of the jars with a clean, damp cloth, and screw on the lids.

6. Process the jars according to the Boiling-Water-Bath Canning instructions on page 158 (20 minutes for both pints and quarts; 25 minutes at 1,001–3,000 feet altitude; 30 minutes at 3,001–6,000 feet; and 35 minutes above 6,000 feet).

7. Remove the jars and adjust the screw bands to tighten the seals.

8. Leave the jars undisturbed for 12 hours to cool. Test the seals. Store in a cool, dry place.

CANNING APPLESAUCE

1. One bushel of apples (42 pounds) will give you 16–20 quarts of applesauce. Wash and quarter the apples. It is not necessary to peel them. Place the apples in a kettle with about 1 inch of water. Cover and cook until soft, stirring occasionally to prevent scorching and to allow the apples to cook evenly.

2. While the apples cook, prepare your jars and lids and preheat water in your canner. Wash the jars and lids in warm, soapy water; rinse thoroughly. Prepare the lids according to the manufacturer's directions.

3. When the apples are soft, press through a sieve, strainer, or food mill to remove the skins and seeds.

4. Return the applesauce to a kettle and bring to a boil. Cook for at least 10 minutes, or until the sauce reaches the desired consistency. Season to taste with sugar and cinnamon, if desired.

BOILING-WATER-BATH CANNING

The U.S.D.A. recommends the following procedure for boiling-water-bath canning for jams, jellies, and such:

1. Fill the canner halfway with water. Preheat water to 180°F.

2. Load filled jars, fitted with lids, into the canner rack and use the handles to lower the rack into the water; or fill the canner, one jar at a time, with a jar lifter.

3. Add more boiling water, if needed, so the water level is at least 1 inch above jar tops. Turn heat to the highest position until water boils vigorously.

4. Set a timer for the recommended processing time. Adjust for altitude.

5. Cover with the canner lid and reduce the heat setting to maintain a gentle boil throughout the process schedule. Add more boiling water, if needed, to keep the water level above the jars.

6. When jars have been boiled for the recommended time, turn off the heat and remove the canner lid.

7. Using a jar lifter, remove the jars and place them on a towel, leaving at least 1-inch spaces between the jars during cooling.

5. Ladle the hot applesauce into clean, hot jars, leaving ½ inch of head-room. Wipe the rims with a clean, damp cloth, and screw on the lids.

6. Process the jars according to the Boiling-Water-Bath Canning instructions on the opposite page (15 minutes for pints and 20 for quarts up to 1,000 feet; 20 and 25 minutes at 1,001–3,000 feet; 20 and 30 minutes at 3,001–6,000 feet; and 25 and 35 minutes above 6,000 feet).

7. Remove the jars. Adjust the screw bands to tighten the seals.

8. Leave the jars undisturbed for 12 hours to cool. Test the seals. Store in a cool, dry place.

FREEZING APPLES

Even if you select only firm, fresh, and flavorful apples for freezing, you will find that they will soften and lose flavor during frozen storage. For that reason, it is important to choose only perfect apples and to refer to the table on page 175 to see which varieties are recommended for freezing. When cooked applesauce is to be frozen, choose those apples listed on the chart under the heading Sauce. Cooking protects the texture and flavor — as long as the sauce is used within a reasonable time.

Try to speed up the freezing process by placing the containers of just-packed fruit next to a freezing surface on the freezer floor or a shelf and leaving space around each one. When the containers of fruit are completely frozen, repack your freezer to its fullest advantage.

Freezing Apple Slices

1. Peel, core, and cut 3 pounds (9 medium) apples into ¼-inch slices.

2. Drop into 1 gallon water mixed with 2 tablespoons lemon juice.

3. Bring a pot of water to a boil and drop in the apple slices, a pound at a time. Blanch for 1 minute only. Drain immediately.

4. Place in single layers on baking sheets and freeze.

5. When frozen, place in plastic freezer bags, seal, and freeze.

Yield: 3 quarts

Freezing Whole Apples

1. Peel and core or wash and core the apples.

2. Drop into a pot of boiling water and blanch for 1 minute.

3. Drain and stuff with a mixture of nuts and raisins bound together with honey.

4. Wrap individually in plastic wrap or wax paper. Place in freezer bags and put into the freezer.

5. To prepare the apples for the table, remove from the freezer and place in a buttered dish, dot with butter, cover, and bake in a preheated 400°F oven for 30 minutes, or until they can be pierced easily with a fork.

Freezing Pies

If you intend to freeze baked pies, make sure they are completely cold before enclosing them in freezer bags. Any heat left in the pie results in condensation in the freezer bag, which causes the pie to become moist and the crust soggy.

Bake frozen in a preheated 375°F oven for approximately 30 minutes. Cover the top with aluminum foil if the crust gets too brown.

Unbaked pies can be assembled as usual, but don't put steam vents in the top crust until you are ready to bake. Bake frozen in a preheated 425°F oven for 30 minutes. Reduce oven to 375°F and bake for 30–40 minutes longer. Cover the crust with aluminum foil if it gets too brown before the pie has finished baking.

Making Jams, Jellies, Butters, and Chutneys

Making preserves is simple, economical, and wonderfully satisfying. I get infinite pleasure from surveying jars of golden apple butters, chunky marmalades, and chutneys. And the clear, vivid green of mint apple jelly is a cause for admiration.

These homemade treasures taste equally good on toast or when accompanying a savory dish.

Of all fruits, tart cooking apples are in a class of their own for jam-making because their high pectin content acts as a natural setting agent.

Just for safety, the U.S.D.A. recommends that all jellies, jams, marmalades, butters, chutneys, and relishes be packed into hot, sterilized jars, leaving ¼ inch of headroom, then sealed according to the jar manufacturer's instructions, and processed for 5 minutes in a boiling-water bath up to 1,000 feet altitude (10 minutes at 1,001–6,000 feet and 15 minutes above 6,000 feet).

Sterilizing Jars and Lids

1. Choose a pan that can be fitted with a false bottom (such as a plate) to prevent the jars from touching the bottom of the pan and cracking, and one that is deep enough to allow the water to cover the jars.

2. Wash the jars and lids in warm water containing a little dishwashing liquid. Rinse thoroughly.

3. Place the jars upright in the water bath and fill with hot (not boiling) water. Continue to fill the water bath until the jars are completely covered. Bring to a boil and boil gently for 15 minutes. (Some dishwashers have a sterilizing cycle you can use to sterilize jars.)

4. Scald or boil the lids according to the manufacturer's instructions only.

5. As the jars are needed for filling, remove from the boiling water (or dishwasher) one at a time.

Apple Butter

To make this in quantity, quadruple the recipe and cook for several hours.

8–9 medium apples (Paula Red, Golden Delicious, Empire, Ida Red, McIntosh, Gala)

1 teaspoon water

1 orange

1 pound (2½ cups) brown sugar

APPLE BUTTER FOR PETE

Environmentalist and folk musician Pete Seeger once asked me to make apple butter at the Clearwater's Annual Pumpkin Sail Festival in Beacon, New York. In one of his letters, he suggested, "We could make the people of the downriver area more conscious of the fact that the Hudson Valley is a great apple-producing region and produces many varieties besides the standard Delicious and Macs." And so we made lots of apple butter.

1. Core and quarter the apples. Place in a large pan, add the water, cover, and simmer on low for 30 minutes, or until soft. Stir the apples halfway through the cooking time.

2. Grate the zest of the orange and reserve in a bowl. Cut the orange in half and squeeze the juice into the zest. You should have ½–¾ cup juice.

3. Press the cooked apples through a sieve. Discard the skins, return the pulp to the pan, and stir in the sugar, grated zest, and orange juice.

4. Simmer over very low heat, stirring frequently, until the mixture is thick — about 1½ hours. (Or pour the mixture into a roasting pan and bake uncovered at 350°F for 1 hour, stirring occasionally. Reduce the oven to 250°F and bake 2–3 hours longer, or until thick.)

5. Sterilize two pint jars. Remove the mixture from the heat and ladle into the hot, sterilized pint jars; leave ¼ inch of headroom. Run a rubber spatula around the inside of the jar to release air bubbles. Wipe the rim of the jar with a clean cloth. Cap each jar as the manufacturer directs. Process for 5 minutes in a boiling-water bath (page 158). Adjust for altitude if needed.

Yield: 2 pints

Joyse's Blackberry and Apple Jam

Breakfast at my mother's Scotland home would not be complete without a dish of this jam to accompany the toast. The blackberries grow in wild abundance behind her house; in August, she gathers them by the pound.

3 medium tart green apples (Granny Smith, Rhode Island Greening, Twenty Ounce, Winesap)

1 cup water

6 cups blackberries

8 cups (4 pounds) granulated sugar

1. Peel, core, and slice the apples. Reserve the peels. Place the slices in a large kettle with ½ cup of the water. Cover and simmer for 15–20 minutes, or until the apples are soft.

2. Place the blackberries in a medium-sized pan and add the apple peels tied in cheesecloth and the remaining ½ cup water. Simmer for 15–20 minutes, or until the fruit is soft.

3. Discard the apple peels. Add the blackberries and liquid to the apples. (Or force the cooked blackberries through a sieve to remove the seeds; add the fruit pulp to the apples.)

4. Stir in the sugar and dissolve over very low heat.

5. Stir the fruit and bring to a rolling boil for 10 minutes, or until the jam sets when dropped onto a chilled saucer.

6. When a set has been reached, remove the mixture from the heat and ladle into four hot sterilized pint jars; leave ¼ inch of headroom. Run a rubber spatula around the inside of the jar to release air bubbles. Wipe the rim of the jar with a clean cloth. Cap each jar as the manufacturer directs. Process for 5 minutes in a boiling-water bath (page 158). Adjust for altitude if needed.

Yield: About 4 pints

Apple Marmalade

*I don't remember ever not eating marmalade — it was
always served at breakfast.*

2 medium oranges
   (1 pound)

2 medium lemons
   (½ pound)

1 grapefruit (½ pound)

6 medium tart apples
   (2 pounds) (Twenty
   Ounce, Rhode Island
   Greening, Granny
   Smith, Winesap)

12 cups water

5 pounds extra fine sugar

1. Scrub the oranges, lemons, and grapefruit. Thinly peel the zest with a potato peeler or paring knife, making sure to avoid the inner white pith. Chop or shred the zest. Place in a large kettle.

2. Squeeze the juice and seeds into a bowl. Cut out the inner membranes; chop coarsely. Tie the fruit and seeds in a doubled piece of cheesecloth. Add the juice to the pan with the zest.

3. Wash, peel, and core the apples. Add the apple peels to the cheesecloth and tie. Add to the kettle. Chop the apples and add to the kettle with the water.

4. Bring to a boil, reduce the heat, and simmer for about 1½ hours, or until the peels are tender and the liquid reduced by half.

5. Lift the cheesecloth bag, squeeze the juice into the kettle, and discard. Add the sugar and stir until completely dissolved.

6. Bring to a boil; boil rapidly until a candy thermometer registers 220°F (about 15–20 minutes), or until the marmalade sets when dropped onto a chilled saucer. Skim off the foam.

7. When a set has been reached, remove the mixture from the heat and ladle into eight hot sterilized pint jars; leave ¼ inch of headroom. Run a rubber spatula round the inside of the jar to release air bubbles. Wipe the rim of the jar with a clean cloth. Cap each jar according to the manufacturer's instructions. Process for 5 minutes in a boiling-water bath (page 158). Adjust for altitude if needed.

Yield: Approximately 8 pints

Mint Apple Jelly

*For cinnamon apple jelly, omit the mint leaves and add
2 cinnamon sticks. A few crab apples in the kettle
provide extra pectin for a good jelly set.*

10   medium tart apples
       (Granny Smith, Jonathan
       or Jonagold)

3   cups water

2   cups fresh mint leaves

3   tablespoons lemon juice

2¾–3   cups sugar

       green food coloring
          (optional)

1. Quarter the apples and place in a large kettle with the water and mint. Simmer for 30 minutes or until the apples are soft.

2. Pour the fruit and liquid into a sieve or colander lined with four layers of cheesecloth, or into a dampened jelly bag, and strain. Allow to drip for 2–3 hours. For a clear jelly, do not press the fruit.

3. Measure the juice into a clean kettle (there should be about 4 cups) and bring to a boil. Add the lemon juice and sugar (¾ cup per cup of juice). Boil for 10 minutes, or until the sugar has dissolved and it registers 220°F on a candy thermometer. The jelly should set when dropped onto a chilled saucer.

4. When the jelly stage has been reached, skim off the foam. Add a drop of green food coloring, if desired.

5. Pour immediately into four hot, sterilized pint jars; leave ¼ inch of headroom. Run a rubber spatula around the inside of the jar to release air bubbles. Wipe the rim of the jar with a clean cloth. Cap each jar according to the manufacturer's instructions. Process for 5 minutes in a boiling-water bath (page 158). Adjust for altitude if needed.

Yield: Approximately 4 half-pints

Rhubarb Apple Chutney

My mother used to make this chutney when she still lived at Woodfalls, her family's farm in Cheshire, England. There was a very large orchard there, and Mother oversaw the making of preserves for home use.

5 medium apples (Fuji, Granny Smith, Tydeman Red, Wellington)

4 pounds rhubarb, cut into 1-inch pieces

4 medium onions, chopped

1 pound dark raisins

1 pound brown sugar

2½ cups malt vinegar

2 teaspoons curry powder

½ teaspoon ground cinnamon

½ teaspoon ground cloves

½ teaspoon ground ginger

½ teaspoon ground mace

¼ teaspoon cayenne pepper

1. Peel, core, and coarsely chop the apples.

2. Place all ingredients in a large kettle, cover, and bring to a boil.

3. Remove the cover, reduce the heat to very low, and simmer, stirring occasionally, for about 2 hours, or until the mixture is thick and tender.

4. Ladle into 7 or 8 hot, sterilized pint jars; leave ¼ inch of headroom. Run a rubber spatula around the inside of the jar to release air bubbles. Wipe the rim of the jar with a clean cloth. Cap each jar according to the manufacturer's instructions. Process for 5 minutes in a boiling-water bath (page 158). Adjust for altitude if needed.

Yield: 7–8 pints

Apple Peach Chutney

Sweet peaches complement the apples' tartness in this fragrant, fruity chutney.

16 medium peaches (about 3 pounds)

8 medium apples (Puritan, Tydeman, Granny Smith)

1 large onion, chopped

1 pound brown sugar

1 pound golden raisins

2 cups cider vinegar

1 tablespoon ground ginger

1½ teaspoons ground cinnamon

1 teaspoon ground nutmeg

½ teaspoon ground cloves

1. Peel, pit, and dice the peaches.

2. Peel, core, and dice the apples.

3. Combine all the ingredients in a large kettle, cover, and bring to a boil.

4. Remove the cover, reduce the heat to very low, and simmer for approximately 2 hours, until the chutney is thick and tender.

5. Ladle into 7 or 8 hot, sterilized pint jars; leave ¼ inch of headroom. Run a rubber spatula around the inside of the jar to release air bubbles. Wipe the rim of the jar with a clean cloth. Cap each jar according to the manufacturer's instructions. Process for 5 minutes in a boiling-water bath (page 158). Adjust for altitude if needed.

Yield: 7–8 pints

MEET the APPLES:
Apple Varieties

DESCRIPTIONS OF THE GENERAL CHARACTERISTICS of apples should be taken as just that — general. Like that of wines, the quality of apples depends on many factors — latitude, terrain, weather, and the care with which they are grown, among others.

Apples of the same variety vary not only from year to year but from day to day, as they mature. I've had apples from the same bag, in fact, that varied widely in appearance and taste. Maybe they were the same shape, but the colors were remarkably different, depending on the degree of ripeness.

The background, or undercast, color of an apple changes from dark green to light green to yellow as it ripens, and the surface turns a bright red or a deeper yellow. In some apples, the surface color completely obscures the background color. Take, for example, one of my favorite apples, the Empire. Sometimes these are all bright red, sometimes bright red on a yellow background. A knockout of juicy spiciness when fully mature, the Empire is flat and uninteresting when eaten before its prime.

Some apples at first look are only a solid green, yellow, or red; but on closer inspection, it can often be seen that they are faintly streaked, marbled, or dotted with a yellow or pink blush. Get to know the apples — from everyday varieties to heirlooms to new hybrids — in the following pages.

Popular Varieties

The following descriptions cover those apple varieties that are the most popular with the orchardists, are good keepers, and are available for several months in a number of U.S. states and Canadian provinces.

Braeburn. Discovered as a seedling in New Zealand in 1952, it is believed to be an offspring of the Lady Hamilton. A yellow-skinned apple blushed with red stripes, Braeburn has pale cream flesh that is crisp, juicy, and sweetly tart. A favorite apple for fresh desserts, it is also good for baking and making into a deliciously sweet applesauce.

Cortland. This apple, a cross between a Ben Davis and a McIntosh, was developed by the New York State Agricultural Experiment Station in Geneva, New York. It entered the commercial market in 1915. Cortlands are grown mainly in the Northeast, the northern Great Lakes states, and eastern Canada. A medium-to-large red-and-green-striped apple, it is crisp, juicy, and sweetly tart. Because its white flesh resists browning, Cortlands are favored for salads and fruit cups. It is also a good all-purpose apple.

Delicious, Golden. Grown in most regions across the country, Golden Delicious is the second-most grown after Red Delicious, to which it is not at all related. The Golden Delicious (or Yellow Delicious, as it is sometimes called) was discovered in West Virginia in 1914, when it was called Mullin's Yellow Seedling. The Stark Brothers, owners of a nursery in Louisiana, Missouri, who specialize in acquiring the rights to new apple varieties, later acquired the Golden Delicious. Sometimes, the Starks have found new varieties through fruit competitions they sponsored. This is a medium-to-large pale yellow or yellow-green apple that is mild and sweet. Although it is crisp when harvested in September and October, its pale flesh often becomes dry and soft. Its skin shrivels when not kept under refrigeration. Particularly desirable for snacks, fresh desserts, and salads, the Golden Delicious is a good all-purpose apple.

Delicious, Red. The Red Delicious is grown throughout the United States and is America's most popularly grown apple. It was called Hawkeye when it was discovered in 1872 in Peru, Iowa, and was renamed Red

Delicious in 1895 by the Stark Brothers. (George Stark is said to have proclaimed, "It's delicious," when he took a bite of Jesse Hiatt's Hawkeye during the judging of his 1895 fruit competition.) This bright red apple is crisp and juicy when harvested in September and October. Although Red Delicious is considered a good keeper by the industry, its sweet and mild-tasting flesh is all too often a mealy, mushy disappointment. It is best used for snacks, salads, and fruit cups.

Empire. A cross between Red Delicious and McIntosh, the Empire was introduced into commercial production by the New York State Agricultural Experiment Station in 1966. Grown mostly in the Northeast and upper midwestern states, this medium, red-on-yellow (sometimes all-red) apple is crisp and juicy. With its sweet and spicy flesh, it is one of the very best for eating out of hand, in salads, and in fruit cups.

Fuji. This flavorful, aromatic apple is the number-one seller in Japan, where it was developed in 1958 by crossing Ralls-Genet and Red Delicious. A pretty apple with yellowish green skin blushed with orange-red stripes, it has dense, crisp, and sweetly tart light yellow flesh. Fuji retains its flavor even when stored at room temperature and develops a better flavor when held in long-term storage. An excellent apple for eating out of hand, adding to salads, and making into applesauce.

Gala. Developed in 1934 in New Zealand by J. H. Kidd of Greytown, Wairarapa, Gala (sometimes called Royal Gala) is a cross of Kidd's Orange Red and Golden Delicious. The thin, red-orange skin — actually red striping over gold — encases aromatic, semisweet, yellowish white flesh. Crisp and juicy, it is a good apple for eating out of hand, using in salads, and pairing with soft, mild cheeses.

Ginger Gold. Ginger Gold was discovered as a seedling in an orchard in Virginia after Hurricane Camille devastated the area in 1969. It is believed to be the offspring of Albemarle Pippin. It is a large apple with greenish gold skin, which is sometimes tinged with a slight blush when fully mature. The crisp, juicy flesh is pure white and resists turning brown for hours after it has been peeled and cut. This combination makes Ginger Gold a good choice for salads, hors d'oeuvres trays, and garnishes. When the apples are first picked, their flavor is tart with a sweet aftertaste, but as they mature under refrigeration, their flesh becomes mellow and honey sweet. Ginger Gold is best eaten within two months of harvest.

Granny Smith. Although one of the most popular varieties sold in the United States, it is imported here year-round from the Southern Hemisphere. Granny Smith originated in Sydney, Australia, about 100 years ago, and is now grown in several states. It is a medium pale green apple that, depending on maturity, is mildly to very tart. It is crisp and firm, and even though it doesn't have great flavor, its rather hard flesh makes it a good all-purpose apple. The U.S. crop is available October through June.

Ida Red. This apple was scientifically developed in 1942 at the University of Idaho Agricultural Experiment Station. It is a cross between a Jonathan and a Wagener. Although it is grown in greatest volume in the northeastern and upper midwestern states, its production is increasing by popular demand throughout the country. It is medium to large, bright red, and has creamy white flesh that is very firm, crisp, and juicy. All-purpose apples, the sweetly tart, deliciously spicy Ida Reds are especially good for snacks and desserts, and their firm quality makes them particularly desirable for baking. The flavor improves after several months in controlled-atmosphere storage.

Jerseymac. A medium-to-large red apple with a green undercast. Its tough skin encases flesh that is tangy, crunchy, and juicy. Although it makes a good all-purpose apple, it does not keep well.

Jonagold. The Cornell University New York State Agricultural Experiment Station developed the Jonagold by crossing Jonathan and Golden Delicious. It was introduced to American consumers in 1968. A large, slightly elliptical apple with yellow skin blushed with faint orange-red stripes, it has flesh that is supercrisp, juicy, and an even balance of sweet and tart. Jonagold is an excellent all-purpose apple, one of the best for eating out of hand.

Jonamac. A small-to-medium, red-on-green apple that is firm, mildly tart, and juicy, this can be considered an all-purpose apple. However, it is not a good keeper.

Jonathan. This was called Rick Apple when it was first introduced in 1826 at Woodstock, New York. Although it is the fifth-largest apple crop in the United States, its production in the North is now limited. It is a medium red apple with an attractive yellow blush. The flesh is firm, crisp, juicy, and sweetly tart, with a spicy aftertaste. A great all-purpose apple that holds its shape well, Jonathan is in demand for baking whole and in pies.

Lodi. A small to medium light green apple, the Lodi has firm flesh that is mildly tart but rather flavorless. It is fine for cooking purposes, but this late summer apple is not a good keeper.

Macoun. A cross between a McIntosh and a Jersey Black, this is a medium red apple that sometimes has an unattractive gray bloom. However, its snow-white flesh is supercrisp and juicy, and its honey sweetness makes up for its mild flavor. This is most desirable for eating fresh, for snacks, salads, and fruit cups. It also makes good applesauce. Macoun is a poor keeper — it gets soft and loses flavor in storage — so it is rarely available after November. It is grown mostly in the Northeast, with limited production in the northern Midwest.

McIntosh. John McIntosh discovered this apple in Ontario, Canada, in 1830. Ranking third in volume in the United States, it is grown throughout the northeastern and upper Great Lakes states, eastern Canada, and British Columbia. It is a medium red-on-green apple, with sweet flesh that is crisp, juicy, and slightly perfumed. Macs are excellent to eat fresh in autumn; later, they are best used for sauce. McIntosh apples collapse when baked whole or in pies.

Melrose. In 1970, the Ohio State Horticultural Society named Melrose the official state apple. It has a somewhat flat shape, and the skin is a dull red on yellow. However, it makes up for its drab appearance with firm, crisp flesh that is sweet, juicy, and flavorful. Melrose is an excellent all-purpose apple.

Mutsu/Crispin. This descendant of Golden Delicious was introduced into the United States by the Japanese in 1948. Although grown mostly in the Northeast, Mutsus are gaining wider popularity. The very large yellow-green fruits are not unlike the Golden Delicious; however, the flesh is much juicier and coarser, and its skin suffers less from storage. It is an excellent all-purpose apple.

Newtown Pippin. Supposedly discovered in Newtown, New York, on Long Island, in 1758, this is one of the oldest varieties to be found in commercial production. It is now grown in several states and is a great favorite with the processing industry — its firm, crisp, juicy, and sweetly tart flesh makes it ideal for pie fillings and sauce.

Northern Spy. This apple originated at East Bloomfield, New York, around 1800. Today, it is grown mostly throughout the Northeast, the northern Midwest, and eastern Canada. This is a medium-to-large apple with a pale green-to-yellow undercast, heavily striped with red. Its mellow, creamy flesh is crisp, juicy, and richly aromatic — qualities that are prized by the commercial processing industry. It is an excellent all-purpose apple and freezes well. Because it is a biennial bearer, Northern Spy is declining in popularity with commercial orchardists.

Patricia. A star. This is so limited in production that it sells out very quickly during the second week of September. One of the very best eaters, but not a good keeper, it is a small, light green and yellow apple splashed with pink. It is crisp, crunchy, juicy, sweet, and tastes of "apple."

Paula Red. This variety was discovered in 1960, in Sparta, Michigan, and introduced commercially in 1967. It is grown mostly in the Northeast and northern Midwest states. A medium, early-September apple, it is usually red, though sometimes shaded with yellow-green. The flesh is crisp, juicy, and sweetly tart. Although Paula Reds are fair all-purpose apples, they are not good keepers and should be used within six weeks or so of harvest.

Puritan. A lemony yellow and pinkish apple that has firm, juicy, and puckery-tart flesh. Puritans are considered fair for all culinary uses except for baking whole.

Raritan. This red-on-green apple has a great "apple" flavor and is one of my all-time favorites. It has wondrously crunchy, juice-spurting flesh that is mildly tart-sweet. It is a great thirst quencher.

Rome Beauty. This large deep red apple was found growing in Rome, Ohio, in 1816. The flesh is sweet, mildly tart, dry, and firm. Although mediocre for eating fresh, Rome Beauties are very good for baking because they retain their shape and flavor. For that reason it remains one of the most popular varieties grown throughout the United States.

Stayman. Stayman apples were discovered in Leavenworth, Kansas, in 1866 and originated from Winesap seeds. For that reason, they are some-times incorrectly called Stayman Winesap. They're grown in the Northeast, eastern Midwest, and South Atlantic states. Stayman is a medium deep red apple, often shaded with green (it sometimes fails to ripen in the Northeast). Its sweetly tart flesh is crisp and juicy and is delicious for eating fresh. It is also a good all-purpose apple.

Tydeman Red. The skin of this red-on-green apple is tough and firm; the rather chewy flesh is on the tart side. It is a good cooking apple.

Wellington. A medium red-and-green apple with firm, somewhat juicy flesh. It is nothing spectacular, but a good all-purpose apple.

Winesap. Thought to have originated in New Jersey in the late 1700s, Winesap is one of our oldest apples still in commercial production (Newtown Pippin is the other). Although it is grown in most apple-produc-ing regions, its heaviest volume comes from the Northwest and the mid-Atlantic states. The Winesap is of medium size, with a thick red skin and crisp, crunchy, and juicy flesh. The flavor is sweetly tart with a winy after-taste. It is an excellent all-purpose apple.

York Imperial. When this apple was first discovered at York, Pennsylvania, around 1830, it was called Johnson's Fine Winter Apple. It is grown in the Appalachian states of Pennsylvania, West Virginia, Virginia, Maryland, and Delaware, and its production volume is high enough to rank sixth in the United States. An apple of medium size with a lopsided shape, it has deep red skin with greenish yellow streaking. York Imperial is a crispy, firm apple that is both sweet and tart, with a somewhat mild flavor, and it is in great demand for commercial processing into pie filling and sauce. It is a good all-purpose apple that mellows in cold storage.

APPLE VARIETIES AND THEIR BEST USES

Variety	Harvest and Availability	Eating	Salad	Sauce	Baking Whole	Pie	Freezing
Baldwin	Nov./April	Good	Good	Good	Good	Good	Fair
Braeburn	Nov./June	Excellent	Excellent	Excellent	Excellent	Excellent	Good
Cortland	Sept./June	Good	Excellent	Good	Good	Good	Fair
Delicious, Golden	Sept./June	Good	Excellent	Excellent	Good	Good	Good
Delicious, Red	Sept./June	Good	Good	Poor	Poor	Poor	Poor
Empire	Oct./June	Excellent	Good	Good	Fair	Fair	Fair
Fuji	Oct./June	Good	Good	Good	Fair	Good	Fair
Gala	Sept./May	Good	Good	Excellent	Good	Good	Fair
Granny Smith	Oct./June	Good	Good	Fair	Good	Good	Good
Ida Red	Oct./March	Good	Good	Good	Excellent	Excellent	Good
Jerseymac	Aug./Sept.	Good	Good	Good	Fair	Fair	Poor
Jonagold	Oct./April	Excellent	Excellent	Good	Good	Good	Good
Jonamac	Sept./Oct.	Good	Good	Good	Poor	Fair	Poor
Jonathan	Sept./April	Excellent	Good	Good	Excellent	Excellent	Good
Lodi	July/Aug.	Fair	Fair	Fair	Fair	Fair	Poor
Macoun	Sept./Nov.	Excellent	Good	Good	Poor	Fair	Poor
McIntosh	Sept./June	Good	Fair	Good	Poor	Fair	Poor
Melrose	Oct./April	Good	Good	Excellent	Excellent	Excellent	Excellent
Mutsu/Crispin	Oct./May	Excellent	Good	Excellent	Good	Excellent	Good
Newtown Pippin	Oct./May	Good	Good	Excellent	Good	Excellent	Good
Northern Spy	Oct./May	Good	Good	Good	Excellent	Excellent	Good
Patricia	Sept.	Excellent	Good	Good	Poor	Fair	Poor
Paula Red	Sept./Oct.	Good	Good	Good	Fair	Fair	Poor
Puritan	Aug./Sept.	Poor	Fair	Fair	Poor	Fair	Poor
Raritan	August	Excellent	Good	Good	Poor	Fair	Poor
Rhode Island Greening	Oct./April	Poor	Fair	Good	Good	Good	Good
Rome Beauty	Oct./June	Poor	Fair	Good	Good	Good	Good
Stayman	Oct./May	Good	Good	Good	Good	Good	Good
Twenty Ounce	Aug./Dec.	Poor	Fair	Good	Good	Good	Good
Tydeman Red	Aug./Sept.	Fair	Fair	Fair	Poor	Fair	Poor
Wellington	Aug./Sept.	Good	Good	Good	Poor	Fair	Fair
Winesap	Nov./July	Excellent	Excellent	Excellent	Good	Good	Good
York Imperial	Oct./June	Excellent	Good	Good	Excellent	Excellent	Good

Hardy Antique Apple Varieties

Thousands of apple varieties evolved in the United States during the 17th, 18th, and 19th centuries when Colonial farmers decided to plant apple seeds instead of the young apple tree shoots, or scions, that were transported from England and the Continent. It was thus they found that the seed of an apple did not produce a tree of the same original variety. It was also during the 18th and 19th centuries that apple seeds were spread from coast to coast by the legendary Johnny Appleseed. Born John Chapman in 1774 in Massachusetts, he traveled the new territories for 40-odd years, selling seeds, cuttings, and plants.

The demise of certain apple strains was inevitable. With thousands of varieties to be eaten and sold, those that spoiled quickly were considered a bad risk. By the turn of the 20th century, when transportation became more reliable and all manner of food was available from different areas of the country and various parts of the globe, the heavy reliance on homegrown and local food was drastically diminished. No longer was the home orchard the main source of fruit. Consequently, it was no longer practical to grow such a wide variety of apple trees that had to be pruned, fertilized, and protected from birds and insects. Only those that produced apples judged to be good keepers, and the best for making pies, sauce, and cider were cultivated. Apples that could not stand up to shipping and long storage were discontinued, as were trees that did not bear their first crop for 10 years, and then only every other year thereafter. Also neglected were those apples with rough, brownish, or mottled skins, deemed to be aesthetically unacceptable to the American public.

Another important element contributed to the elimination of some apple varieties. In 1918, the ravages of a severe winter took their toll on thousands of apple trees in the East. In starting over, commercial orchard growers followed the recommendations of pomologists and planted an abundance of McIntosh, Red Delicious, Golden Delicious, and Rome Beauties. However, such old-time favorites as Wealthy, Tolman Sweet, Pound Sweet, Rhode Island Greening, and Baldwin can still be found in some of the smaller commercial orchards whose clientele is local rather than nationwide.

Indeed, I consider it a lucky day when I stumble upon an old-fashioned orchard, where the gardener prefers flavor to abundance. Such varieties can be a revelation — not only in taste, but also in name and appearance.

Ashmead Kernel. This apple was raised around 1700 by Dr. Ashmead in Gloucester, England. Considered one of the finest dessert apples, the sugary sweetness is deliciously tempered with a touch of acid in the juice. Adding to this wonderful flavor, the slightly green, yellow flesh is crisp and aromatic. Ashmeads, somewhat lopsided and conical in shape, have golden-bronze russet skin blushed with orange.

Baldwin. This apple originated in Wilmington, Massachusetts, around 1740. Grown mostly in New York State and New England, it is no longer popular with commercial growers because it takes about 10 years to bear fruit, and then does so only biannually. It is a large red apple, streaked with yellow. The flesh is firm, crisp, juicy, moderately tart, and aromatic. This is a good all-purpose apple.

Black Gilliflower or Sheepnose. This apple, discovered in Connecticut in the late 1700s, has the shape of a sheep's nose and deep, purple-red skin. The flesh is firm, sweet, and fragrant. It is delicious for eating out of hand, and can also be used for baking.

Black Twig. Sometimes spelled Blacktwig, this apple is also known as Twitty's Paragon. Discovered as a seedling around 1830 on the farm of Major Rankin Toole in Fayettville, Tennessee, it was distributed by Twitty's nursery. In the 19th and early 20th century, Black Twig was a popular variety with orchardists in Central Virginia. Considered a good keeper, this juicy and aromatic apple needs some storage time for its yellow flesh to develop the best flavor. The attractive skin is usually yellow striped and blushed with dark red.

Chenango Strawberry. This originated in New York state in the mid-1800s, and is a pale yellow apple with pink stripes. The soft flesh has a distinct strawberry fragrance.

Cox Orange Pippin. "Pippin" was a common term for a small apple when this one originated in England around 1830. It is wonderfully aromatic, with a rather rough, deep yellow skin that is splashed with orange and red. The flesh is crisp, tender, and fragrantly juicy, making it one of the best dessert apples. It also makes choice cider.

Duchess of Oldenburg. First imported to England in 1815 from Russia, this apple was brought to the United States in 1835. Its tender, red-striped skin encases yellow-tinged flesh. Crisp, firm, and juicy, it is highly rated for pies and sauces, but considered too tart for eating out of hand.

Fameuse or Snow. Originating in France, this has been grown in New York and Vermont since around 1700. It is small and firm, with bright red, sometimes purple, skin. Its snow-white, crisp flesh may be striped with red. Excellent for eating raw in desserts and salads, it does not hold its shape during cooking.

Lady. This small apple originated in France during medieval times. With its red and green skin and firm, crisp, white flesh, it is very much in demand around the Christmas season for table decorations. It is delicious to eat fresh and makes good cider.

Porter. A large yellow apple splashed with red, it originated in Massachusetts around 1800. Its firm, white flesh is crisp, tender, and flavorful. It is ideal for canning, cooking, and eating raw.

Pound Sweet or Pumpkin Sweet. This apple originated in Connecticut around 1850. It is very large, with green-on-yellow striped skin. The flesh is yellow and juicy, with an unusual and rather sweet flavor. It is good for baking.

Red Astrachan. This apple reached the United States from Russia around 1835. Its pale yellow skin is splashed with bluish red stripes, and the juicy, white flesh is often tinged with red. An early-summer apple that ripens unevenly and does not keep well, the Red Astrachan is used for cooking before it is fully mature. However, when ripe, it is excellent for eating fresh in desserts and salads.

Rhode Island Greening. This variety originated around 1700 from a chance seed found growing outside a Rhode Island tavern owned by a Mr. Green of Green's End, Newport. The bright green skin surrounds flesh that is crisp, juicy, and tart. If allowed to ripen, it becomes mellow enough to be eaten out of hand. However, most orchardists pick them "green," which makes them a perfect pie apple.

Roxbury Russet. A real American oldie that originated in Roxbury, Massachusetts around 1635. Its gold skin is mottled with flecks of brown and red; the crisp yellow flesh is deliciously sweet. Excellent for eating fresh and making into cider, it also has a long storage life.

Smokehouse. William Gibbons grew this apple near his smokehouse during the early 19th century in Lancaster County, Pennsylvania. Its yellowish green skin is mottled with red and the creamy flesh is firm and juicy, making it a good candidate for fresh desserts and the salad bowl. It is not recommended for cooking.

Sops of Wine. With white, red-flecked flesh that resembles bread dipped in wine, this apple has a pedigree that goes all the way back to medieval England.

Summer Rambo. One of the older varieties, it originated in France, where it was called the Rambour France, and was introduced into the United States in 1817. This large apple is greenish yellow with red stripes. The tender, juicy flesh makes it ideal for eating fresh and making into sauce.

Tolman Sweet. This apple is said to have originated in Dorchester, Massachusetts, around 1822. Its greenish yellow skin is sometimes blushed with light pink. The white flesh is exceptionally sweet and it is considered the best for making naturally sweet applesauce. It is also good for baking and eating fresh.

Tompkins King. Discovered in New Jersey around 1800, it is a large, yellow apple splashed with broad red stripes. The skin is tender and the creamy flesh crisp, juicy, and moderately tart. Not a favorite for eating fresh, it is best used for cooking.

Twenty Ounce. It was first exhibited in Massachusetts around 1845, and is thought to have originated in Connecticut. This is a large green apple splashed with red stripes when ripe. Its firm, tart flesh is encased in tough skin. This combination makes it superb for cooking.

Wealthy. This thin-skinned, pale yellow apple, heavily shaded with red, was discovered in Minnesota around 1860. Its crisp, juicy white flesh is often streaked with red. It's an excellent apple for eating fresh, for cooking, and for making cider.

Westfield Seek-No-Further. At one time considered the finest of dessert apples, this one originated in Westfield, Massachusetts, around 1796. The skin of this yellowish green apple is splashed with red, and the pale yellow flesh is crisp, juicy, and flavorful.

Winter Banana. Over 100 years old, this variety originated in Indiana. It has pink-on-yellow cheeks and, not surprisingly, a flavor reminiscent of bananas.

Wolf River. Named after Wolf River in Wisconsin, where it was found, this apple is thought to have originated in 1880. It is an oversized apple, and stories abound in which only one apple was necessary for a whole pie. Its skin is pale yellow, heavily streaked with red, and the light yellow flesh is firm, tender, and juicy. It's excellent for eating fresh and cooking.

APPENDIXES

APPLE INFORMATION AND SOURCES

Apple Councils & Organizations

U.S. Apple Association
703-442-8850
www.usapple.org
The links page provides contact information for U.S. state and regional apple organizations.
Note: The U.S. Apple Association (formerly the International Apple Institute), based in McLean, Virginia, is the national trade association representing all segments of the apple industry, including the 9,000 apple growers located throughout the country.

Experimental Orchards

These orchards are among those producing new hybrid and/or heirloom apple varieties.

Applesource
1716 Apples Road
Chapin, IL 62628
800-588-3854
http://applesource.com
Applesource has stopped selling apples and are now focusing on apple processing tools. For apples, see Doud Orchards.

Breezy Hill Orchard & Cider Mill
828 Centre Road
Staatsberg, NY 12580
845-266-3979
www.hudsonvalleycider.com

Doud Orchards
8971 North State Road 19
Denver, IN 46926
www.doudorchards.com
"The same folks who have been shipping apples for Applesource since 1986, will continue to ship the same high quality fruit you've come to expect when you've ordered from Applesource."

Hollabaugh Bros., Inc.
545 Carlisle Road
Biglerville, PA 17307
717-677-9494
www.hollabaughbros.com

Linden Vineyards
3708 Harrels Corner Road
Linden, VA 22642
540-364-1997
www.lindenvineyards.com

Salinger's Orchard
230 Guinea Road
Brewster, NY 10509
845-277-3521
www.salingersorchard.com

METRIC CONVERSION

Unless you have finely calibrated measuring equipment, conversions between U.S. and metric measurements will be inexact. It's important to convert the measurements for all of the ingredients in a recipe to maintain the same proportions as the original.

General Formula for Metric Conversion

Ounces to grams	multiply ounces by 28.35
Grams to ounces	multiply grams by 0.035
Pounds to grams	multiply pounds by 453.5
Pounds to kilograms	multiply pounds by 0.45
Cups to liters	multiply cups by 0.24
Fahrenheit to Celsius	subtract 32 from Fahrenheit temperature, multiply by 5, then divide by 9
Celsius to Fahrenheit	multiply Celsius temperature by 9, divide by 5, then add 32

APPROXIMATE METRIC EQUIVALENTS BY VOLUME

U.S.	METRIC
1 teaspoon	5 milliliters
1 tablespoon	15 milliliters
⅓ cup	60 milliliters
½ cup	120 milliliters
1 cup	230 milliliters
1¼ cups	300 milliliters
1½ cups	360 milliliters
2 cups	460 milliliters
2½ cups	600 milliliters
3 cups	700 milliliters
4 cups (1 quart)	0.95 liter
1.06 quarts	1 liter
4 quarts (1 gallon)	3.8 liters

APPROXIMATE METRIC EQUIVALENTS BY WEIGHT

U.S.	METRIC	METRIC	U.S.
¼ ounce	7 grams	1 gram	0.035 ounce
½ ounce	14 grams	50 grams	1.75 ounces
1 ounce	28 grams	100 grams	3.5 ounces
1¼ ounces	35 grams	250 grams	8.75 ounces
1½ ounces	40 grams	500 grams	1.1 pounds
2½ ounces	70 grams	1 kilogram	2.2 pounds
4 ounces	112 grams		
5 ounces	140 grams		
8 ounces	228 grams		
10 ounces	280 grams		
15 ounces	425 grams		
16 ounces (1 pound)	454 grams		

APPLES FOR GOOD HEALTH

"An apple a day keeps the doctor away" may not just be folk wisdom. Apples are an excellent source of dietary fiber and pectin, which help lower blood sugar, reduce cholesterol, and inhibit certain types of cancer. Today, researchers know that apples (including 100-percent apple juice and apple-sauce) also contain high levels of flavonoids and antioxidant phytonutri-ents — nutrients that are found exclusively in plants. According to the National Institute for Cancer, the American Heart Association, and the American Diabetes Association, recent health studies are proving that increased consumption of fruits and vegetables, especially those containing flavonoids and antioxidant phytonutrients, helps protect against heart dis-ease, fight diet-related cancers, and reduce hypertension and diabetes. The results of the following studies were reported from 1997 to 2000:

- In 1997, a 24-year study by Finland's National Public Health Institute reported that a flavonoid-rich diet, particularly flavonoid quercetin from apples, was associated with a 46-percent reduced risk of developing cancer.
- Another 25-year study by Finnish researchers concluded that the flavonoid quercetin found in apples and onions was directly associated with the lowest risk of coronary mortality.
- British researchers made a five-year study that indicated that people who ate several apples every week had better lung func-tion than non–apple eaters.
- In 1999, the University of California-Davis reported that a labo-ratory study showed that the antioxidant phytonutrients found in apples and apple juice help protect against cardiovascular dis-ease by fighting the "bad" LDL type of cholesterol.
- In 2000, Finnish researchers reported the results of a 28-year study, which determined that those individuals who ate the most apples had the lowest risk of thrombotic stroke.
- In June 2000, Cornell University researchers reported that apple phytonutrients inhibited the growth of colon cancer and liver cancer cells in laboratory studies.

INDEX

Note: Page numbers in **boldface** refer to tables.

Other Storey Titles You Will Enjoy